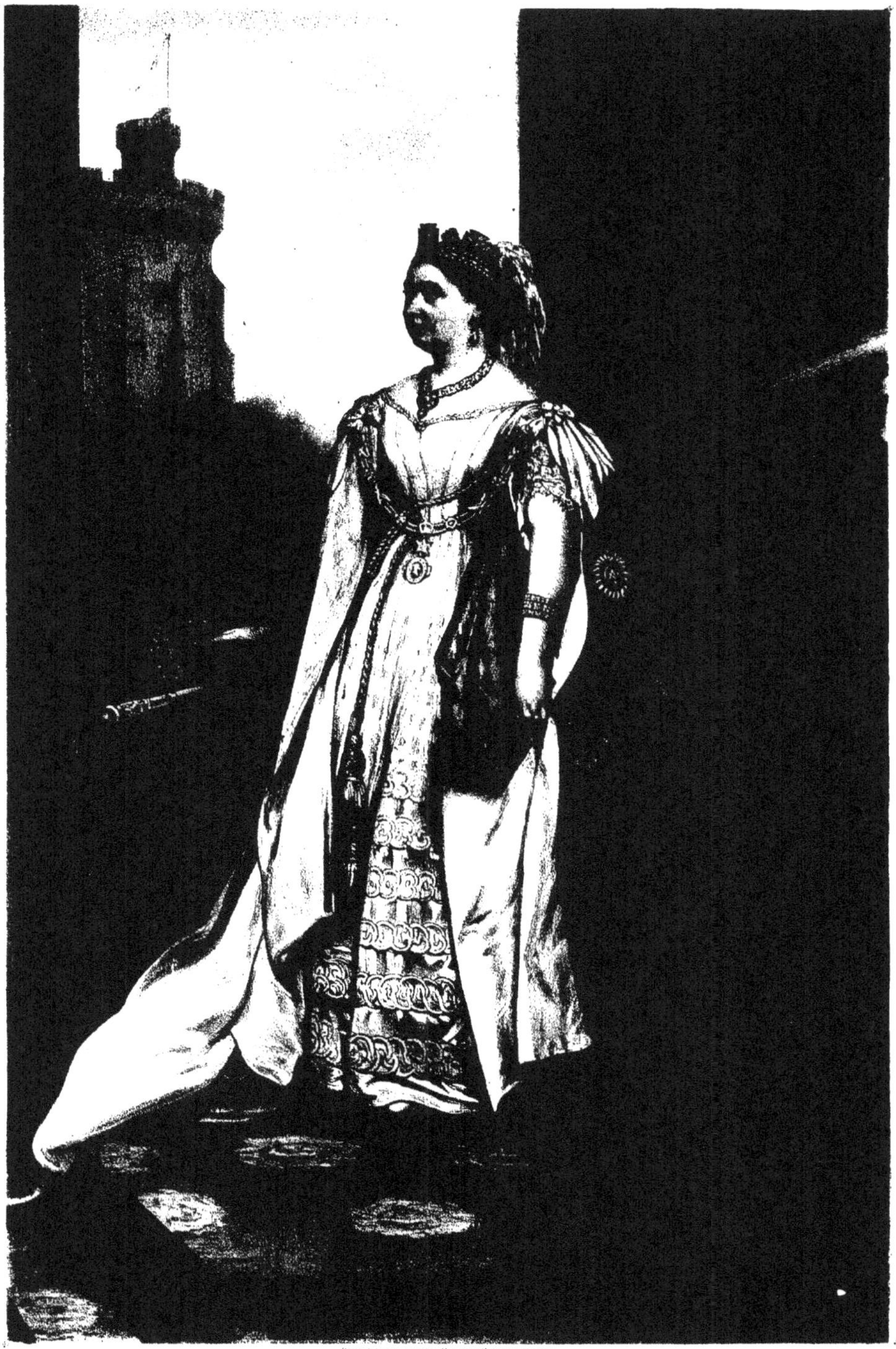

DRAWN & LITHOGRAPHED BY MACLURE & MACDONALD LONDON

VICTORIA, EMPRESS OF INDIA.

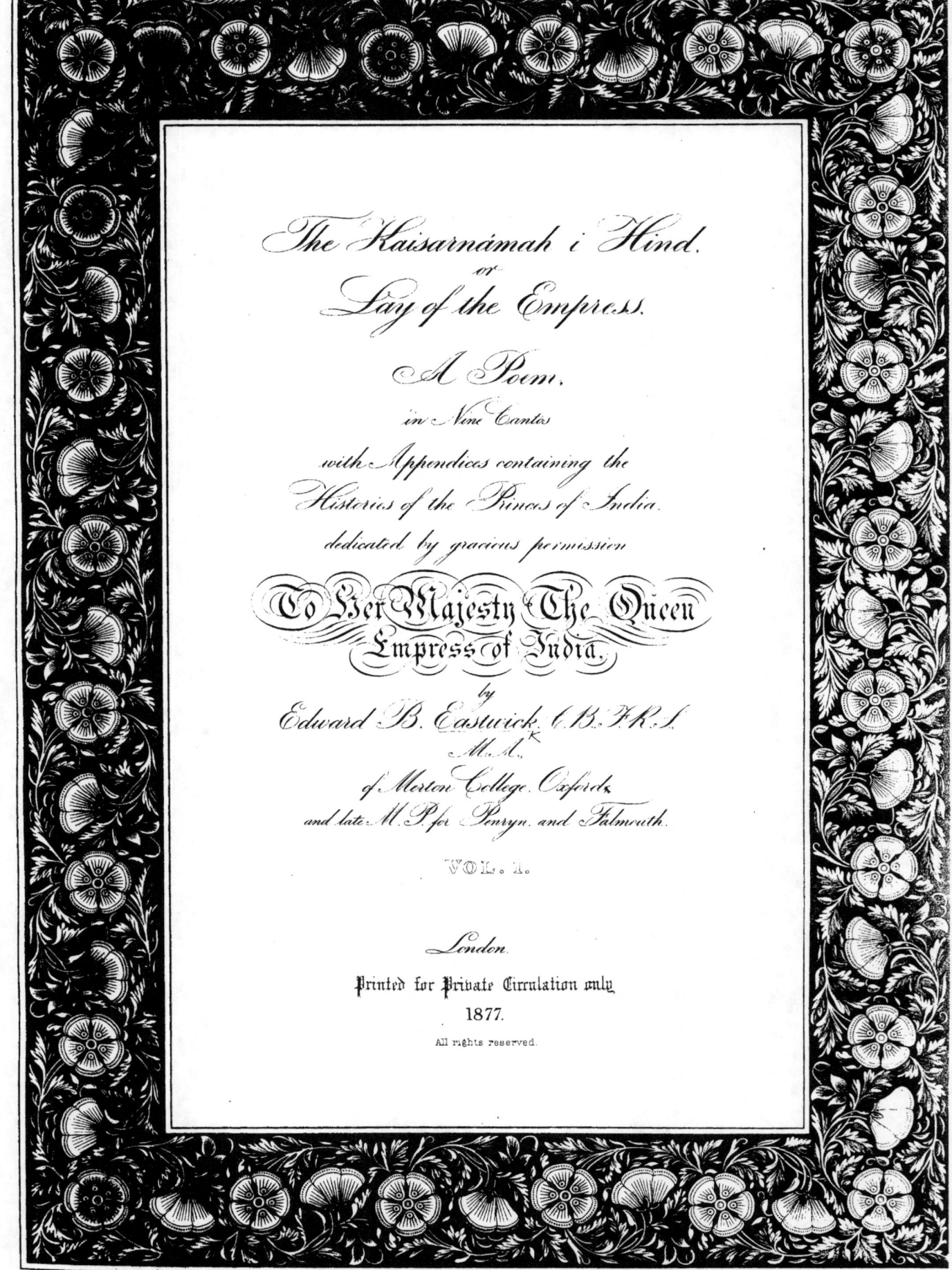

The Kaisarnámah i Hind,
or
Lay of the Empress.

A Poem,
in Nine Cantos
with Appendices containing the
Histories of the Princes of India,
dedicated by gracious permission

To Her Majesty The Queen Empress of India,

by
Edward B. Eastwick, C.B., F.R.S.,
M.A.,
of Merton College, Oxford,
and late M.P. for Penryn and Falmouth.

VOL. I.

London.
Printed for Private Circulation only
1877.
All rights reserved.

The Royal Arms of England.

Dedication to Her Most Gracious Majesty Queen Victoria, Empress of India.

Madam,

It is now nearly a quarter of a century since your Majesty graciously condescended to accept the dedication of my version of the celebrated Persian work, called the Anvár-i-Suhailí. The intrinsic merits of that remarkable composition inspired me with hope, that even in the less attractive form of a Translation, it might be viewed with favor by your Majesty, but in presenting this original Poem I have no such confidence. The subject of your Majesty's proclaimed accession to the Imperial sway of an Empire greater than that of Timúr, is indeed one worthy to be sung by the most illustrious of Poets, but I feel that I can offer nothing worthy of acceptance, except the expression of the most devoted loyalty, a feeling which is shared by all your Majesty's subjects as well in India as in England.

Madam,

Your Majesty's most faithful and obedient Servant and subject,

Edward B. Eastwick.

PREFACE.

Long before I was informed that Mr. Talboys Wheeler had been instructed to prepare an official account of the important ceremony and magnificent spectacle which marked the assumption of the title of Empress of India by Her Majesty the Queen, I had resolved to write on the subject. Mr. Wheeler in his exhaustive compilation has supplied all that the public can desire to know as to the official details of what then took place, and it will be seen that it is not my particular object to tread on the ground which he has so well and completely occupied. My efforts are directed to supply, in addition to a poetical description of the Imperial assemblage, a careful history of the princely families of India, a work which has never been attempted as a whole. In the First Volume will be found, in Appendix A, a History of the Nizáms of the Dakan, whose dominions were at one time equal in extent to the territory of a first-rate European State, and are still very much larger than those of most of the sovereigns of Europe of the second rank. In this history I have translated, and somewhat condensed, the whole of the *Hadíkah i Álam*, a Persian MS. composed by Mír Álam, the well-known Minister of the Nizám who accompanied the Duke of Wellington, then Colonel Wellesley, to Seringapatam. The only part of that work that I have omitted is that which relates to the History of the Dakan before any member of the family of the Nizám came upon the scene. Much interesting matter will be found in this work, which, as far as I am aware, has never before been read by any European, at all events has never been translated into English. For proof of the interest attaching to this work I will content myself by pointing to the testamentary instructions of the great Nizámu-'l-mulk to Násir-jang, his son and successor, in which he speaks of the offer of the throne of Dihlí made to him by Nádir Sháh, and declined for reasons there assigned. The *Hadíkah i Álam* has been supplemented from various histories, and now, with Colonel Hastings Fraser's excellent work entitled, *Our Faithful Ally*, forms a complete chronicle of the Nizáms of the Dakan.

In the Second Volume, which will be in English and Hindí, will be given the History of the Marátha Princes and the Rájahs of Rájpútáná, and in the Third, in English and Sanskrit, that of the Sikh Chiefs and the other principal ruling Houses of India.

I have now to record my grateful thanks in the first place, to His Excellency Lord Lytton, Viceroy of India, who generously approved of a work which I dare not venture to hope has any merit beyond such traces as may be found in it of patient and faithful labour, and recommended it to the gracious notice of Her Majesty the Queen.

In the next place I desire to mention His Excellency Sir Sálar jang the Regent for, and Prime Minister of, His Highness the Nizám, to whose kind assistance I owe more than I can express.

I have also to acknowledge, with gratitude, the assistance I have received from Colonel Davies, C. S. I., Commissioner of Dihlí, but for whose hospitality I should not have been enabled to witness the assemblage at Dihlí, which I have here attempted to describe. Colonel Davies also obtained for me the cooperation of the Poets, and Khush Nawísán, who translated into Persian, and wrote out in a beautiful Persian hand my Poem. The Núwáb Ziyau-'d-dín Khán Bahádur, who is the most famous Poet of India now living, superintended the Persian translation, which was made chiefly by Amír Ján. To Mr. John Murray I have to express my thanks for his kind permission to copy a Map of the Marches of Alexander, contained in his excellent classical Atlas. I am also under much obligation to Messrs. Bourne and Shepherd, Messrs. Elliott and Fry, Messrs. Lock and Whitfield, the London Stereoscopic Company, and many other well-known Photographers, who have permitted me to make use of their admirable Photographs of Indian Scenery, and of various distinguished personages. Lastly, I have to express my grateful acknowledgments to the Princes, Noblemen, and Gentlemen whose names are given below, by whose subscriptions I have been enabled to publish this First Volume and hope to bring out the remaining Volumes of this most costly work.

EDWARD B. EASTWICK.

London, *August* 1, 1878.

LIST OF SUBSCRIBERS

TO THE

KAISARNÁMAH I HIND

AND

DISTRIBUTION OF COPIES.

PRESENTATION COPIES	10
RESERVED FOR THE SUPREME GOVERNMENT OF INDIA	10

SUBSCRIBERS.

	COPIES
The Right Honourable the Lord Cranbrook, Secretary of State for India	1
The Right Honourable the Earl of Northbrook, G.C.S.I., late Viceroy of India	1
H.H. Mír Mahbúb Alí Khán Bahádur Fath jang, Nizámu 'd daulah, Nizámu 'l mulk, Rustam i daurán, Aristú i zamán, Muzaffiru 'l mamálik, Ásif jáh	2
H.E. the Núwáb Mukhtáru 'l mulk, Shujau 'd daulah, Sir Sálár jang Bahádur, G.C.S.I., Regent of the Nizám's Dominions	1
H.H. the Mahárájah Siwáí Rám Sing Bahádur of Jaipur, G.C.S.I.	3
H.H. the Mahárájah Tukají Ráo Holkar Bahádur, G.C.S.I.	2
H.H. the Mahárájah of Kashmír and Jamun, G.C.S.I.	1
H.H. the Maháráo Rájah Mangal Sing Bahádur of Alwar	1
H.H. the Mahárájah Jaswan Sing Rájah of Ratlám	1
H.H. the Mahárájah Jaswant Sing Bahádur of Bhartpúr, G.C.S.I.	1
H.H. the Mahárájah of Travancor, G.C.S.I.	2
H.H. the Ráo of Kachh	1
H.H. the Mahárájah of Cochin	1
H.H. Mahárájah Cham Rájendra Wadíar Bahádur, the Mahárájah of Maisúr	1
H.H. the Mahárájah Ishwarí Prasád Náráyan Sing Bahádur of Paráras, G.C.S.I.	1
H.H. the Mahárájah of Bijánagar	1
H.H. the Mahárájah of Vijyanagaram, K.C.S.I.	1
H.H. the Mahárájah of Bardhwán	1
H.H. the Mahárájah of Johore, K.C.S.I.	1
H.H. Prince Ikbálu 'd daulah	1
H.H. the Núwáb Sádík Muhammad Khán Bahadur of Bháwalpur	1
The Royal Asiatic Society of Bombay	1
H.H. Núwáb Khairu 'n nissá Bígam Sáhibah, widow of His late Highness Núwáb Ghulám Muhammad Ghaus Khán, Núwáb of the Karnátik	1
H.H. Azimu 'n nissa Bígam Sáhibah, widow of His late Highness Núwáb Ghulám Muhammad Ghaus Khán, Núwáb of the Karnátik	1
The Honourable Mír Humáyún Jáh Bahádur, Member of the Legislative Council of Madras	1
The Mahárájah of Venkatagiri, C.S.I.	1
Sir Jamshídjí Jijibháí, Bart., C.S.I.	1
Sir Albert Sassoon, K.S.I.	1

H.H. the Rájah of Pudukottah	1
The Honourable G. N. Gajpati Ráo, Member of the Legislative Council of Madras	1
Sir Kaúsji Jahángír Readymoney	2
Sir Mangaldas Náthubhái, Kt., C.S.I.	1
Dínshah Mánikji Petit, Esq., J.P.	1
N. Mánikji Petit, Esq.	1
Ardashír Hormazdji Wadia, Esq.	1
Kesauji Naik, Esq.	1
Bahrámji Jijíbhái, Esq., C.S.I.	1
The Honourable Sorábji Shahpúri Bangáli	1
Varjíwandás Mádhudás, Esq.	1
Murárji Gokaldás, Esq.	1
Tapidás Varjdás, Esq.	1
Seth Govindás, C.S.I., of Mathura	1
Kaúsji Naushírwánji Bhandúpwála	1
Captain Eastwick, late Member of the Council of India	1
Lestock Reid, Esq., C.S., Revenue Commissioner of Belgáon	1
Messrs. Bourne and Shepherd	1

NAMES OF SUBSCRIBERS SUBSEQUENTLY RECEIVED.

His Grace the Most Noble the Duke of Buckingham and Chandos, Governor of Madras	1
The Government of Madras	2
H.H. the Gáekwár, Máhárájah of Baroda	2
Her Highness the Princess of Tanjúr	1
H.H. the Núwáb of Júnágarh	1
H.H. the Thákúr of Bhaunagar	3
H.H. the Jám of Nowanagar	1
H.H. the Máhárájah of Drángdra	1
H.H. the Máhárájah of Gondal	1
W. P. Andrew, Esq., Chairman of the Sindh, Panjáb, and Dihlí Railway	1
Lieut.-Colonel Sir J. M. McGarel Hogg, Bart., K.C.B., M.P.	1
H.H. the Zamorin of Kálikod (Calicut)	1
The Honourable the Rájah of Pithápuram, Member of the Legislative Council of Madras	1
Gawríshankar Udeshankar, Esq., C.S.I., Díwán of Bhaunagar	1
Shámaldás Parmánandás, Esq., of Bhaunagar	1
H.H. the Máhárájah of Morvi	1
H.H. the Máhárájah of Rájkot	1
H.H. the Máhárájah of Kolhápúr	1
H.H. General the Máhárájah Sindhia, Máhárájah of Gwáliár, G.C.B., and G.C.S.I.	1
H.H. the Rájah of Limri	1
H.H. the Rájah of Wadwán	1
Reserved for the Council of India	10

LIST OF ILLUSTRATIONS.

PORTRAITS.

HER MOST GRACIOUS MAJESTY QUEEN VICTORIA, EMPRESS OF INDIA.

THE MOST HONOURABLE ROBERT ARTHUR TALBOT GASCOIGNE CECIL, MARQUIS OF SALISBURY, K.G.,
H.M.'s Secretary of State for Foreign Affairs, late Secretary of State for India.

THE MOST HONOURABLE GEORGINA CAROLINE, MARCHIONESS OF SALISBURY, C.I.
i.e. (A Lady of the Imperial Order of the Crown of India.)

HIS EXCELLENCY EDWARD ROBERT LYTTON, LORD LYTTON,
Her Majesty's Viceroy and Governor-General of India, Knight Grand Cross of the Most Honourable Order of the Bath, Grand Master and Knight Grand Commander of the Most Exalted Order of the Star of India, and Grand Master of the Order of the Indian Empire.

THE RIGHT HONOURABLE EDITH, LADY LYTTON, C.I.,
i.e. (A Lady of the Imperial Order of the Crown of India.)

THE MOST NOBLE RICHARD PLANTAGENET CAMPBELL, DUKE OF BUCKINGHAM AND CHANDOS,
Knight Grand Commander of the Most Exalted Order of the Star of India and Companion of the Order of the Indian Empire, Governor of the Presidency of Madras.

LADY MARY TEMPLE NUGENT BRYDGES CHANDOS GRENVILLE, C.I.,
i.e. (A Lady of the Imperial Order of the Crown of India.)

SIR PHILIP EDMOND WODEHOUSE,
Knight Grand Commander of the Most Exalted Order of the Star of India, and Knight Commander of the Most Honourable Order of the Bath, late Governor of the Presidency of Bombay.

H.H. MÍR MAHBÚB ALÍ KHÁN BAHÁDUR FATH JANG,
Nizamu'd Daulah, Nizamu'l Mulk.

H.E. THE NÚWÁB MUKHTÁRU'D DAULAH SIR SÁLÁR JANG BAHÁDUR, G.C.S.I.,
Regent of H.H. the Nizam's Dominions.

PHOTOGRAPHED VIEWS.

THE TOMB OF SHAHÁBU'D-DÍN, DIHLÍ.
THE TOMB OF THE EMPEROR TUGHLAK, DIHLÍ.
THE HALL OF THE 66 PILLARS, DIHLÍ.
THE TOMB OF SAFDAR JANG, DIHLÍ.
MAUSOLEUM OF THE EMPEROR HUMÁYÚN, DIHLÍ.
TOMB OF NIZÁMU'D-DÍN, DIHLÍ.
THE CHÁNDNÍ CHAUK, DIHLÍ.
THE JAMA MASJID QUADRANGLE, DIHLÍ.
THE JAMA MASJID, DIHLÍ.
THE INTERIOR OF THE DÍWÁN I KHÁS, DIHLÍ.
THE MOTÍ MASJID, DIHLÍ.
THE BRIDGE AND FORT OF SALÍMGARH, DIHLÍ.
ST. STEPHEN'S MEMORIAL CHURCH, DIHLÍ.
THE PURÁNÁ KILA, OR OLD FORT, DIHLÍ.
THE LÁHÚR GATEWAY, DIHLÍ.
THE RIDGE, FROM THE JAMA MASJID, DIHLÍ.
THE KASHMÍR GATE, DIHLÍ.
THE LÁT, OR STONE PILLAR OF FIRÚZ SHÁH, DIHLÍ.
THE KUTB MINÁR, DIHLÍ.
THE KUTB MINÁR, DIHLÍ.
(SHOWING THE CARVING ON THE FIRST GALLERY.)
GENERAL VIEW OF THE GREAT DARBÁR AT DIHLÍ, 1st JANUARY, 1877.
SIR SÁLÁR JANG'S PALACE.

PALACE OF THE NIZÁM AT HAIDARÁBÁD.
THE BRITISH RESIDENCY AT HAIDARÁBÁD.
GOLKONDAH TOMBS.
GOLKONDAH FORT.
GENERAL VIEW OF THE CAVES OF AJANTA.—No. 2.
AJANTA.—FACADE OF VIHÁRA CAVE I, A.D. 500.
AJANTA.—VERANDAH OF CAVE I, A.D. 450.
GENERAL VIEW OF THE CAVES OF AJANTA.—No. 1.
AJANTA.—FRONT OF VIHÁRA CAVE II.
AJANTA.—VIHÁRA CAVE VII, A.D. 100 TO 200.
AJANTA.—FACADE OF CHAITYA CAVE IX, B.C. 100.
AJANTA.—INTERIOR OF CHAITYA CAVE X, B.C. 150—200.
AJANTA.—VERANDAH OF CAVE II, ABOUT A.D. 400.
AJANTA.—INTERIOR OF CHAITYA CAVE XIX.
AJANTA.—FACADE OF CAVE XIX.
AJANTA.—FACADE OF CHAITYA CAVE XIX, A.D. 400—500.
AJANTA.—PORTION OF THE FRONT OF VIHÁRA CAVE XX, A.D. 600.
AJANTA.—FRONT OF VIHÁRA CAVE XXIII, A.D. 500 (?)
AJANTA.—INTERIOR OF CHAITYA CAVE XXVI, A.D. 500—600.
FRONT OF VIHÁRA CAVE XXIV.
FACADE OF CHAITYA CAVE XXVI, A.D. 400—500.

LAY OF THE EMPRESS.

INTRODUCTION.

Canto I.

1

Half girt with giant mountains, on whose crest,
By man untrodden, sleep eternal snows;
Half guarded by a troubled sea's unrest,
And torrents that their barrier waves oppose,
India would seem itself a semi-world,
Safe from attacks without, supplied within,
So needing not its flag should be unfurled
New lands beyond its natural bounds to win,
And wake its borders' peaceful echoes with war's din.

2

And had the Hindús' 'Holy Land' been one,
Their Áryávartta' by one will been swayed,
No pallid children of the western sun
Had dared its radiant confines e'er invade.
The thunder of its war-steeds' trampling then
Had drowned its foemen's feeble battle-cry,
Its countless hosts had thronged each pass and glen,
And left invaders scarce the room to fly,
Room only where they stood to yield, or fight and die.

CANTO I.

3

But 'stead of union discord grew amid
Scenes which love's birthplace might full well have been,
So direful beasts in that fair land are hid,
Where wild flowers bloom and leaves are ever green.
In vain the gods, as Áryan[2] legends tell,
Descended in the twilight hours of man,
As mortals, though immortal, there to dwell.
They came not but to lead the battle's van,
And with their coming war and India's woes began.

4

Yet, disunited, India oft repelled
Invading hosts—e'en Philip's conquering son[3]
Scarce passed its barriers, scarce the prize beheld,
But turned, and left the rich reward unwon.
Too vast the conquest was, or seemed to be,
E'en for Sikandar, fated though to draw
Life's sparkling waters, that none else may see,
Imprisoned deep in gloomy caves, where awe
And silence keep the Maker's mandate without flaw.

5

Where rapid Beah meets her sister flood
His sullen legions paused—obeyed no more
Their leader's voice—the victor vanquished stood,
And sighed to find his dream of conquest o'er.
And where he failed could others hope success?
Ages went by and on that spot again
The war-cloud darkly gathering thundered, Yes!
Strange that on that same Beah-watered plain[4]
Should India's bravest fly, and choke the stream with slain.

THE MOST HONOURABLE ROBERT ARTHUR TALBOT GASCOIGNE CECIL,
MARQUIS OF SALISBURY, K.G.,
H.M.'s Secretary of State for Foreign Affairs, late Secretary of State for India.

CANTO I.

6

But, ere that crowning victory, full oft
Invasion o'er the barrier rivers led
Her hosts, and held her meteor flag aloft,
Till terror to the distant Ganges spread.
And first Menander reached that sacred stream,
And Grecian arms, victorious, sparkled fair
In the pure wave; then faded in the gleam
Of Scythian watch-fires, when their fatal glare,
Seen first on Jhelam's banks, advancing reddened there.

7

Then rose the Star of Islám, Mahmúd came,
Its Angel, and the Messenger of Death;
Before him terror, and around him flame,
All nature drooping withered at his breath.
And where his war-steed trampled nought ere grew:
As on and on his blood-stained way he cleft
'Twas vain to combat, and as vain to sue,
Alike of pity and of fear bereft,
He found a smiling garden, and a desert left.

8

Say, then, ye Wise! whence is this mockery
That man should write in blood the way to Heaven?
Truth is divine, and needs no panoply
To do its work, and human reason leaven.
Is God a God of love? and must we learn
At the sword's point His laws, and are we bound
To teach them so, or may we best discern
Them from example, deeds where love is found?
Surely Truth's mission should with flowers, not thorns, be crowned.

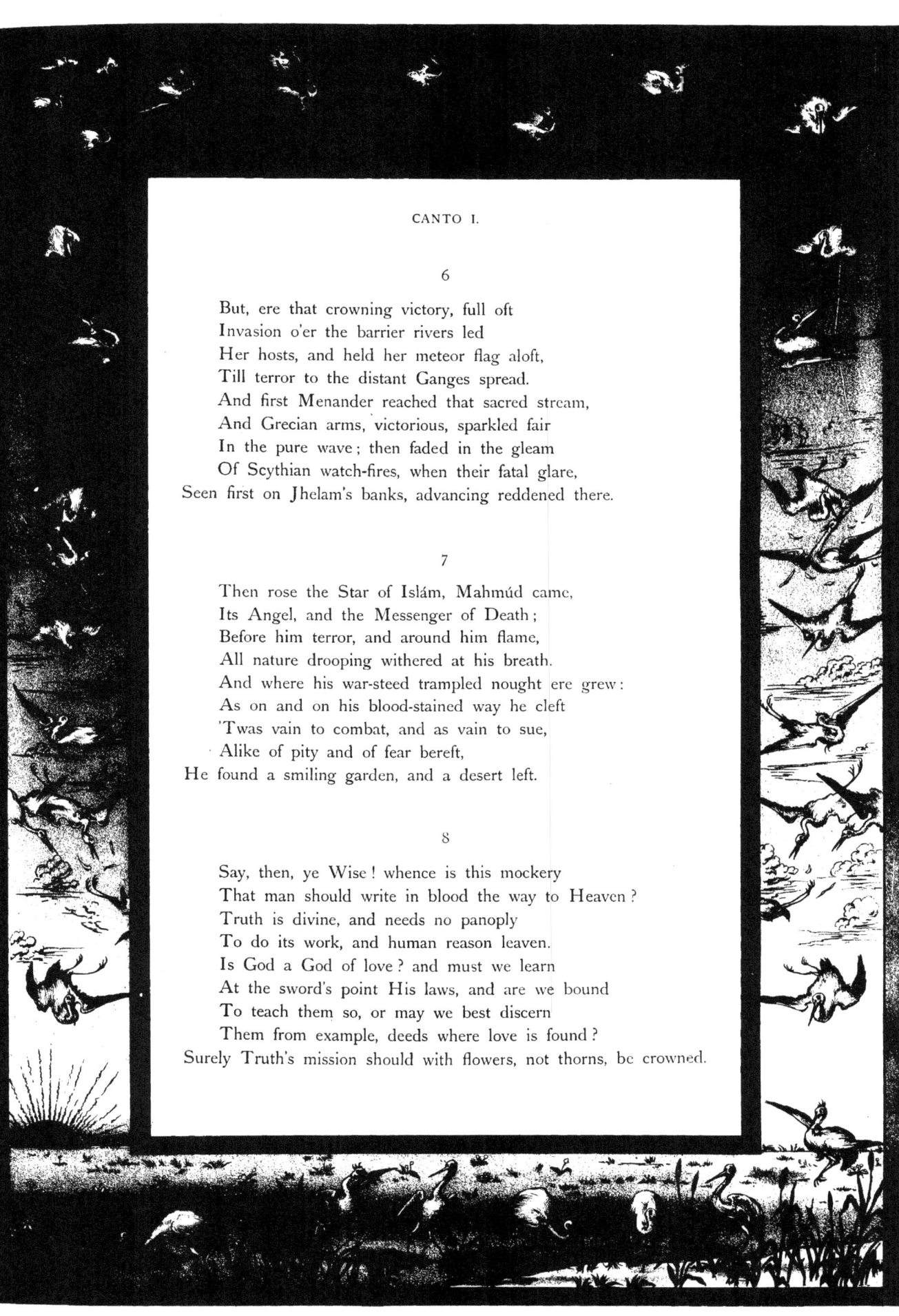

THE MOST HONOURABLE GEORGINA CAROLINE, MARCHIONESS OF SALISBURY, C.I.
i.e. (A Lady of the Imperial Order of the Crown of India.)

CANTO 1.

9

And yet thorns were its crown long since, and are,
And blood of teachers, or of taught, must flow;
Who would teach peacefully their own peace mar;
The peaceful who would learn must suffer woe.
Oh, cruel Paradox! Tears are joy's seed,
And Peace is sown with blood of martyrs—Yes!
Those who love life and peace themselves must bleed,
And through affliction we must learn to bless.
Death is the gate of Life! Hope's root is bitterness!

10

Akbar! to thee alone the praise is due,
That men might doubt or question and dispute
On things beyond this world's imperfect view,
E'en in thy presence, and their conscience suit
With that which brought conviction as their creed.
Aye! thou wert truly great, thy sons not so,
They would be bigots, and they had their meed.
Their palaces are vacant, and weeds grow
Where glittered once all wealth the earth could show.

11

Well! let them pass—their rule could not bestow
That which their country needed, concord, rest,
The calm of power that needs no outward show,
And all that makes a peaceful nation blest.
Those blessings were to come, but tarried long,
Tarried till thought of better things was dead,
Till by prescription Right gave place to Wrong,
And Virtue sighing from the land had fled,
Then Light from Darkness dawned, and Hope her pinions spread.

THE TOMB OF SHAHÁBU'D'DÍN, DIHLÍ.

THE TOMB OF THE EMPEROR TUGHLAK, DIHLÍ.

CANTO I.

12

Marátha, Mughul, and Pathán, all failed
To free their country from its load of ill,
Nor art, nor courage, nor e'en prayer availed,
But high and higher grew the tempest still.
Then came the fatal palsy of despair,
When helmsmen shrink, and let the vessel drive,
And all is dark, nor guiding star is there,
Nor light, but when the clouds red flashes rive,
Then faint the timid, and the bravest cease to strive.

13

At such a moment came unhoped release,
From a far land it came beyond the sea;
'Twas England bade the stormy billows cease
To rage, and set long suffering India free.
Call it not conquest, that which joined Two Lands,
Home of one Race, though parted through long years,
Nor War, that which has ended with clasped hands,
Nor strangers, those who mingle joys and tears;
'Tis Union that survives all hate, and doubts, and fears.

14

Nor heed the shallow Sceptic, when he prates
Of a blind chance that rules our destinies;
Or of the restless atom, that creates
All change, and all things underlies.
Say was it chance, or movement to and fro
Of blind corpuscles, that when India's self
Could find no medicine for its self-made woe,
Sent a few ships and traders to seek pelf,
And end by giving Tímúr's kingdom to a Guelf!

CANTO I.

15

Rather than such dull dreams believe the strife
Of Surs and Asurs, and that ocean churned
Gave forth the amrit,[6] "Nectar," Source of life,
And poison that the throat of Shiva burned.
For life to India from the sea has come,
And Truth is Falsehood's poison, which must slay
All that the old world deified, strike dumb
Its oracles, and make its creeds decay;
Till there arise new light, the light of perfect day.

16

In sooth it was not chance, nor lack of skill
Or daring deeds, and of ambition less,
That India ne'er became one empire; 'twas the will
Of Heaven, that none might alter or transgress.
Akbar had kingcraft and his grandson[7] art,
Nádir was lion-hearted, but none made
Complete the conquest, still some distant part
Refused the yoke, nor Delhi's lord obeyed,
Nor were its armies e'er beneath one flag arrayed.

17

Far stand the Rocks apart on which are graved
Asoka's Edicts,[8] and broad realms between
Were subject to him, but the flag that waved
At Plassey, and on Kábul's heights was seen,
Has long to North and South those limits past,
And lands to East and West more distant won.
Words rock-engraven through long years may last,
But more enduring is that glorious One,
Victoria; writ all realms, all mankind's hearts upon.

THE HALL OF THE 66 PILLARS, DIHLÍ.

THE TOMB OF SAFDAR JANG, DIHLÍ.

CANTO I.

18

Yes! Fate kept back this Eastern diadem,
As though it shone too bright for mortal brow;
Kings sought to wear it, but 'twas not for them,
Thou England's Queen art worthy, only Thou!
Talk not of conquerors, they are often found,
Not so a conqueror, who is all beside
That graces human nature; search earth round,
Show, if thou canst, a better daughter, bride,
And mother, and a heart more tender and more tried.

19

But some, perhaps, may ask—Of what avail
Is this vast empire to the little Isle
That spots the sea, where light and sunshine fail,
Beyond which Life and Nature cease to smile?
Take then for answer—that this empire cost
The priceless blood of heroes, shed like rain,
To win and keep it. Let not that be lost,
For which a thousand hecatombs were slain
Of gallant men—Give not a nation's life in vain.

20

Is glory nothing? Is a golden chain
Of great achievements, with a hundred links
Of victory, sparkling through long years, no gain?
No heirloom to a people? He who thinks
Such glory worthless must possess a soul
No nobler than the clay its tenement.
Why argue then? Enough! put by the scroll
Of England's fame. 'Tis useless to resent
Instincts that formed to grovel are therewith content.

MAUSOLEUM OF THE EMPEROR HUMÁYÚN, DIHLÍ.

TOMB OF NIZÁMU'D·DÍN, DIHLÍ.

CANTO I.

21

What made the Spartan? but the memory
Of glorious deeds by his forefathers done.
What lesson like thy name, Thermopylæ?
Could one who died there have a coward son?
And so the kinsman, or compatriot,
Of one who fought at Delhi, or Assaye,
Could ne'er by panic that proud scutcheon blot,
Or turn from tenfold odds in fear away,
And stain by shameful flight the memory of that day.

22

Then who would wish the ancient curse renewed
That scattered mankind o'er the untilled earth?
When severance first begot mistrust and feud,
And long estrangements to fierce hate gave birth.
Nations are wiser now, they coalesce;
To be one Ruler's subjects makes men friends;
Union is strength and peace and happiness;
And with confederation discord ends.
'Twas an ill spirit parted men, 'tis Love that blends.

23

These are the days of Giant States! 'Tis ill
For dwarfs to dwell with giants, lest one blow
Should crush them, or mere movement chance to kill.
England with all she rules need fear no foe;
Alone she would be dwarfed beside a Power
That now o'ershadows and may soon extend
O'er half two Continents. This is the hour
For smaller states to league, not lose a friend,
Lest when the Balance turns all hope of safety end.

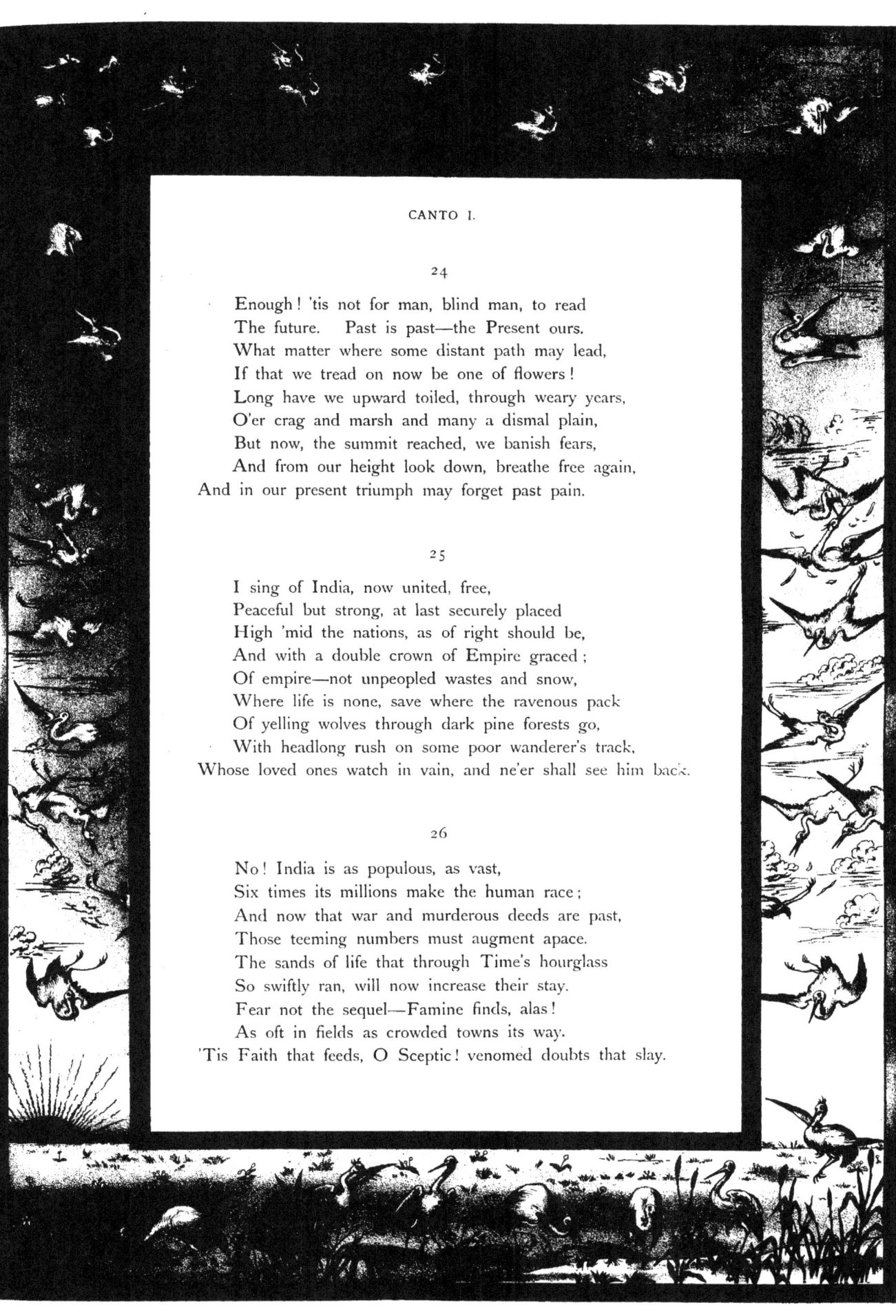

CANTO I.

24

   Enough! 'tis not for man, blind man, to read
   The future.   Past is past—the Present ours.
   What matter where some distant path may lead,
   If that we tread on now be one of flowers!
   Long have we upward toiled, through weary years,
   O'er crag and marsh and many a dismal plain,
   But now, the summit reached, we banish fears,
   And from our height look down, breathe free again,
And in our present triumph may forget past pain.

25

   I sing of India, now united, free,
   Peaceful but strong, at last securely placed
   High 'mid the nations, as of right should be,
   And with a double crown of Empire graced;
   Of empire—not unpeopled wastes and snow,
   Where life is none, save where the ravenous pack
   Of yelling wolves through dark pine forests go,
   With headlong rush on some poor wanderer's track,
Whose loved ones watch in vain, and ne'er shall see him back.

26

   No! India is as populous, as vast,
   Six times its millions make the human race;
   And now that war and murderous deeds are past,
   Those teeming numbers must augment apace.
   The sands of life that through Time's hourglass
   So swiftly ran, will now increase their stay.
   Fear not the sequel—Famine finds, alas!
   As oft in fields as crowded towns its way.
'Tis Faith that feeds, O Sceptic! venomed doubts that slay.

CANTO I.

27

In one pellucid drop, one sunbeam, live
A myriad wondrous creatures, joyous, gay.
Can He Who made them, and Who feeds, not give
Thee and thy children bread, weak doubter, say?
Accept the truth, and think how, day by day,
India's Life-stream is swelling to a sea,
Which might, if numbers count, half Asia sway,
And menace others more than menaced be,
At least be sure of resting glorious, great and free.

28

With such a people, and a realm so grand,
What could a ruler hope or wish for more?
But bounteous Nature has shed o'er the land
Each several blessing of its varied store.
What plains so rich as those the Ganga laves?
What valley like that of thy Lake, Kashmír!
Bright gleams thy fairy city 'mid the waves,
A Venice, mirrored in the waters clear;
And Love's own dwelling[9] sleeps in flowers and foliage near.

29

O'er emerald turf the Chinárs throw their shade,
In terrace over terrace from the Lake.
O Garden of the Breezes![10] thou wert made
That man might pine no more for Eden's sake;
White peaks around, like giant warders, rise,
The silver Lake reflects them as they kiss
The yielding bosom of the cloudless skies,
What charm is wanting to a scene like this!
And Woman fairest here, augments, not mars, its bliss.

CANTO I.

30

Earth can no Eden like this Valley show,
Yet in the midmost heights, in every glade,
That sleeps between thy chains, Abode of Snow!
Beauty 'mid fruits and flowers a home has made
For man, her votary, till uprise sublime
Those vast unconquered and scarped solitudes,
Like the Eternity that limits time,
Upon whose secrets mortal ne'er intrudes,
But Mystery folds her pinions dark and Silence broods.

31

Fit emblem are those Hills, as height o'er height,
They rise from the deep valleys to the sky,
Of England's march from low estate to might,
Till those must perish who would mount as high.
Slow was the progress and the struggle rude,
Since rose the Factory[11] by the Taptí's flood,
To battles when the Khálsa's armies strewed
The plains where Macedonian altars stood,
While the Five Rivers reddened with their champions' blood.[12]

32

But redder flowed the streams, and fiercer blazed
The death-fires, when Rebellion drew the sword,
And the scant loyal band beheld amazed,
The blood of helpless wives and babes outpoured,
Their comrades, traitors, and their homes in flame;
While thronging thousands thought to set their feet
On England's honour, and stamp out her name,
But Vengeance swiftly brought their guerdon meet,
And England's banner rose untarnished by defeat.

THE CHANDNI CHAUK, DIHLI.

THE JAMA MASJID QUADRANGLE, DIHLI.

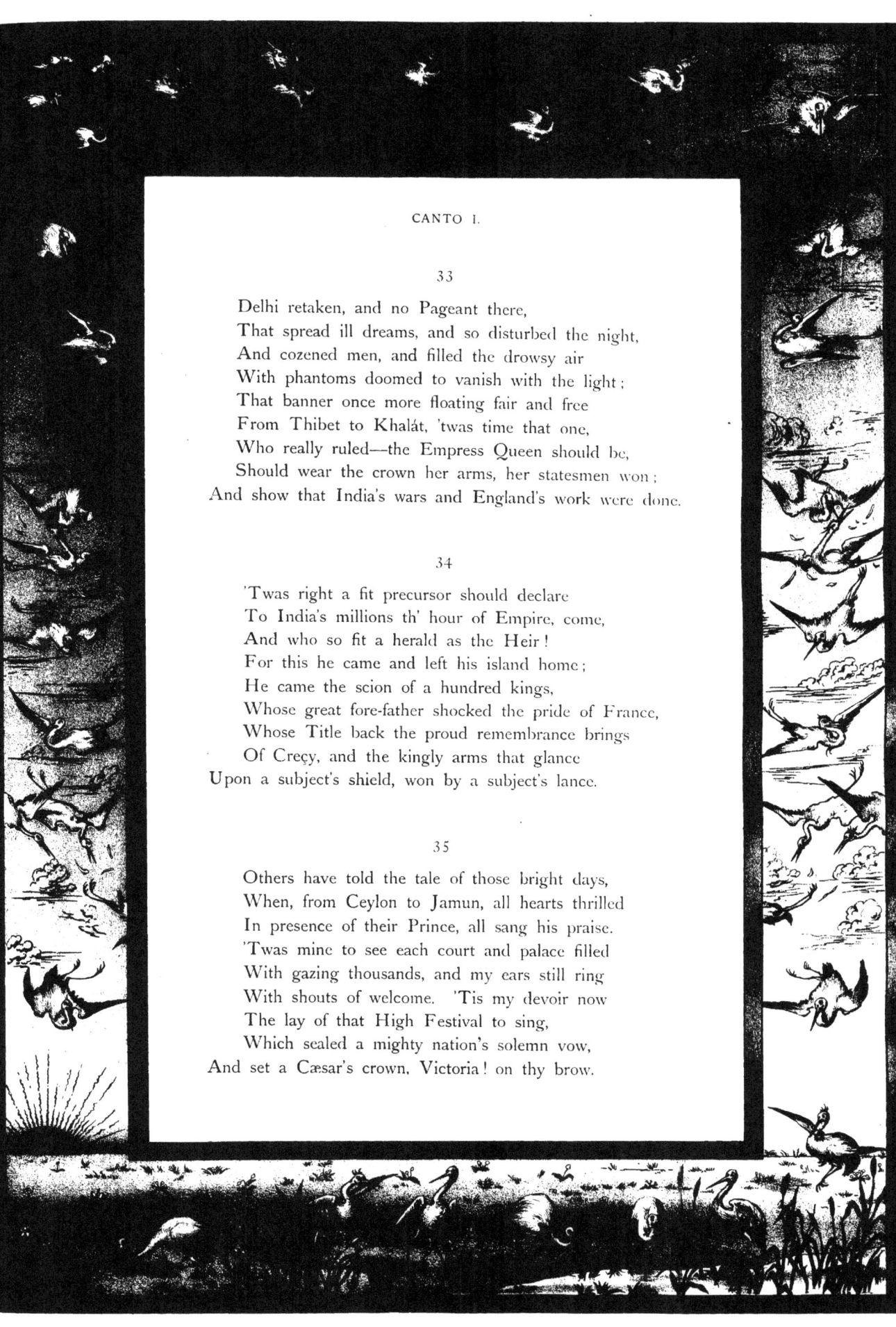

CANTO I.

33

Delhi retaken, and no Pageant there,
That spread ill dreams, and so disturbed the night,
And cozened men, and filled the drowsy air
With phantoms doomed to vanish with the light;
That banner once more floating fair and free
From Thibet to Khalát, 'twas time that one,
Who really ruled—the Empress Queen should be,
Should wear the crown her arms, her statesmen won;
And show that India's wars and England's work were done.

34

'Twas right a fit precursor should declare
To India's millions th' hour of Empire, come,
And who so fit a herald as the Heir!
For this he came and left his island home;
He came the scion of a hundred kings,
Whose great fore-father shocked the pride of France,
Whose Title back the proud remembrance brings
Of Creçy, and the kingly arms that glance
Upon a subject's shield, won by a subject's lance.

35

Others have told the tale of those bright days,
When, from Ceylon to Jamun, all hearts thrilled
In presence of their Prince, all sang his praise.
'Twas mine to see each court and palace filled
With gazing thousands, and my ears still ring
With shouts of welcome. 'Tis my devoir now
The lay of that High Festival to sing,
Which sealed a mighty nation's solemn vow,
And set a Cæsar's crown, Victoria! on thy brow.

Canto II.

THE IMPERIAL ASSEMBLAGE.

1

India! what wanderer o'er thy vast extent
Could call thee less than Empire? If that name
Betoken rule and realm preeminent,
Then mayest thou fitly that proud title claim.
For Europe's kingdoms would but ill compare
With thee, nor e'en its empires half suffice [13]
As rivals thy high dignity to share;
Thrice art thou greater and more peopled thrice;
Their diadems are rich, but thine beyond all price.

2

England did rightly, therefore, to decree
That thou should'st take the rank that is thy due;
That England's Queen thy Empress-Queen should be,
And all the claims of Tímúr's House renew
On grounds more just, for England's Queen bears sway
O'er India's whole expanse, from shore to shore,
And India's countless millions hailed the day,
When seas should part the Sister States no more
At least in heart, and fears and doubts for aye be o'er.

THE JAMA MASJID, DIHLÍ.

THE INTERIOR OF THE DÍWÁN I KHÁS, DIHLÍ.

CANTO II.

3

But whence proclaim these tidings to the world
Of a new Empire linked to this fair isle?
Where should the Flag of Union be unfurled,
And the new Golden Age begin to smile?
A hundred lands that honour might contest,
A hundred cities for that grace contend—
Those which have England's cause supported best,
Or those whose glories from long years descend,
The brave, illustrious foe, or ever-constant friend.

4

Should Agra or Lahore, by Milton sung,
Be chosen for the Field of Jubilee?
Where Akbar reigned, or whence the Khalsa sprung,
The first of India's kings and chivalry?
Or central Ujjain, once Avanti named,
More famous twenty centuries since, than now?
Brave Vikram! when thy era was proclaimed,
When Delhi to thy lance was forced to bow.
Of India's ancient heroes, best and foremost thou!

5

Or Mathura, the birthplace of a god,
Where frolic Krishna with the Gopís strayed,
And danced ecstatic on the verdant sod,
Linked hand in hand with many an amorous maid?
Himself, divinely multiplied, to each
A separate lover seemed, his soft voice charmed
Each fair one, and his glances seemed to teach
Those tender transports that each bosom warmed;
Or, feigning slight, each jealous, loving heart alarmed.

CANTO II.

6

Dear are those woods, those streams to the Hindú.
And dear those legends to the pilgrim throng,
To them no spot so sacred, nought so true
As tales that to that land of dreams belong.
But thrice a thousand years have passed away,
Since Krishna's mirthful rule on earth began,
And Reason shines now with severer ray,
And sterner thoughts engage the soul of man,
And famed must be the spot that leads all India's van!

7

Delhi! the naming thee sums up all claims,
All that past glory, or hoar age, can urge.
A lengthened history thine of famous names,
Of Pæans blending with th' heart-thrilling dirge,
Of thrones of gold, and measureless delights,
Of shrieks of death and madness of despair,
Tales more enchanting than the Thousand Nights,
Sights more appalling than the grave laid bare,
All that can touch the soul, or teach mankind, is there.

8

There Sháh Jahán in peerless splendour throned
Filled up the sparkling measure of his bliss.
And poets gazing on his glory owned,
"If Eden be on earth 'tis this! 'tis this!"
There cruel Nádir grimly scowling saw
The golden city given to sword and shame;
His vengeance then was Delhi's only law,
Unmoved he sat 'mid blood and shrieks and flame;
No tears, no prayers could move him, and no terrors tame.

CANTO II.

9

Last scene of all, the darkest, and the worst,
Was in that hour of bloodshed and dismay,
When fiendish Treason showed its face accursed,
And gave to Guilt the guiltless for a prey.
Yes! Memory well may falter and grow pale,
And the historic Muse shrink back appalled,
Pass with quick step from so abhorred a tale,
Or mute with shame and horror stand enthralled,
Point to the crime and pause till vengeance be recalled.

10

The air was still, the English banner hung
Unmoved on Delhi's lofty battlement,
And to its staff in folds down drooping clung,
Like weary warrior with the battle spent.
There was no sound within the fortress wall
Since boomed with sullen roar the morning gun.
On moat and tower and mosque and marble hall
Poured down the fiery radiance of May's sun;
All seemed at peace, and all men's hearts at one.

11

Stretched on his cot the swarthy Spáhí slept,
With England's honour trusted to his arm;
The sheltered sentry watch half dreaming kept,
No thought had he of danger or alarm.
Few were the English in that citadel,
Weak women most, or children weaker still,
Some gallant men, who served their country well,
That country that, too blind to coming ill,
Left them without support to bide foul Treason's will,

THE MOTI MASJID, DIHLI.

THE BRIDGE AND FORT OF SALÍMGARH, DIHLÍ.

CANTO II.

12

But who be these that come at headlong speed,
Their spurs all bloody and their steeds all foam?
Who follows where such frantic riders lead?
They rode all night, shall morning see them home?
Yes! morning sees them hurtle o'er the bridge,
And Delhi now their lasting home shall be.
Go count the graves along the Western ridge,
There shall the meet reward of treason be.
They fight for freedom—well! they shall for aye be free.

13

The bridge of boats is passed, its keeper slain,
His house flames out—On to the Palace now!
The aged, trembling king forbids in vain,
His English suppliants fall—It is the vow
Of those that served the English; man and maid
Alike must perish—She with golden hair,
He, young and brave, in death together laid.
The Spáhis shout is "Cursed be those that spare!"
It is their Carnival, and Death must revel there.

14

And have these murderous men our horsemen been?
Sworn to the English flag? Aye! even so!—
False to their salt, their oath, their flag, their Queen,
They pay for kindness with the assassin's blow,
The treason spreads, the city's up, bázár
And prison send their butchers. Last the troops
Join in the fray; a fray no more—a war,
And low and lower still our banner droops,
'Twas raised in Glory, and alas! to Treason stoops.

CANTO II.

15

Read out the Roll of Traitors—Third—Eleventh,
Twentieth, and Thirty-eighth, and Fifty-fourth,
The Seventy-fourth, and the Artillery Seventh,
And every armed man from South to North
Of Delhi's plain—Enough! for Delhi 's lost!
And countless cities in their turn rebel:
We would be trustful—trusted, to our cost,
And men shall long the bloody sequel tell,
We lived in a Fool's Paradise—and made a Hell!

16

And should not these things blacken Delhi's name?
That there no festival should e'er be known,
But rather sackcloth spread in sign of shame,
That the false city might its acts atone?
Not so—We suffered wrong and foul despite,
Dark was the crime, and worse than fiends the foe,
But sharp too, was the punishment, and bright,
Aye! more than glorious was his overthrow;
And should that famous record be forgotten.—No!

17

E'en at the outbreak there were noble deeds
That Sparta might be proud of, or old Rome;
There Beresford's heroic lady bleeds,[14]
But first she drives her deadly spear-thrust home.
Calm at their work the fated printers[15] sit,
'Mid shouts of death and burning houses' glare,
They print their latest "Extra," sure that it
Would reach, when they lay gashed and weltering there!
And yet no word, nor gesture showed their mute despair.

ST. STEPHEN'S MEMORIAL CHURCH, DIHLÍ.

THE PURÁNÁ KILA, OR OLD FORT, DIHLÍ

CANTO II.

18

Noblest of all! lo, where the gallant Nine,[16]
Against an army stand to their defence!
They point the cannon, arm the deadly mine,
And smile at baffled Treason's impotence.
On rush the infuriate crowd, whole regiments come,
They mount the wall to crush those dauntless few,
And still as beats to arms the maddening drum
O'er dead and dying they the attack renew,
And fiercer grows the fight where none for mercy sue.

19

And now the Arsenal is almost won,
Again they plant their ladders, climb the wall,
And shout to see the fight must soon be done,
As faint with wounds the brave defenders fall.
One moment and the struggle will be o'er,
Then comes a flash, earth heaves, and buildings rock,
All sounds are swallowed in one deafening roar,
The Magazine explodes with earthquake shock,
Down reel the walls, and ruined heaps the entrance block.

20

Four only of the Nine were left, and they,
Begrimed with smoke, and bruised in every limb,
Emerged slow tottering from the night to day,
With brain confused and tortured eyeballs dim,
Those four were saved—the others perished—not
Their fame—that lives and shall for aye live on,
Until the name of Delhi be forgot,
And the last remnant of its walls be gone;
Time hath no veil to cast such heroes' fame upon.

THE LAHUR GATEWAY, DIHLÍ.

THE RIDGE, FROM THE JAMA MASJID, DIHLÍ.

CANTO II.

21

They were not unavenged—for each that died
A hundred foes were slain, some upward cast,
Some lifeless dashed to earth, and far and wide
The air rained death, and ruin rode the blast.
Live! with this memory too each noble act
By Indians done, who our poor wanderers saved,
Who sheltered those the fierce pursuers tracked,
And for sweet Mercy's sake, their vengeance braved.
Long may those deeds in grateful English hearts be graved!

22

Nor let those faithful Spáhís be forgot,
Who followed through all risks our fortunes still,
Who, spite of creed and country, cast their lot
With England's, and defied their brethren's will.
Live, too, the memory of those gallant men,
The champions of the North, who brought us aid,
To hold the Ridge, till victory smiled again,
And Delhi had its debt of vengeance paid.
Long may beneath our Flag such heroes be arrayed!

23

And could we of our soldiers stint the praise
Who fearless fought 'gainst tenfold odds so long,
Hoped against hope for weary nights and days,
And still repulsed the rebels' baffled throng?
Pour from the cup of their immortal deeds
Deep draughts of Lethe to forget ills past,
Their glory all the infamy exceeds,
That treason on the rebel city cast:
Why think on gloomy scenes, when triumph comes at last!

CANTO II.

24

And so 'twas fixed that Delhi's plain should be
The Place of Concord and Assemblage, where
Should be proclaimed the Imperial dignity,
And India's myriads in the Pageant share,
A Pageant and a solemn conclave too,
Where every Chief and Prince and Potentate
Should to his Queen and Empress homage do:
Thus India would become at length one State,
An Empire undivided, glorious, strong, and great.

25

Wide is that plain—with many a lesson fraught
Of the inconstancy of human things
Built on Time's shifting sands—a truth here taught
By crumbling monuments of ancient kings,
Whose very names are lost; by citadels,
Whose vast enceinte has now become the lair
Of savage beasts; by mosques, whose ruin tells
Decay is not averted e'en by prayer;
By the wild flowers that grow where lived and loved the Fair.

26

North of those ruins—to the eastward swept
And guarded by the Jamna's mighty stream,
The Palace stands, where Sháh Jahán once kept
His court, the heart's delight, the poet's dream.
A hundred feet its giant gateways rise,
Wide is the moat, and high and strong the wall,
And with the first a second rampant vies
In heaven-kissing towers and bastions tall:
Between them all is life, a peopled city all.

THE KASHMÍR GATE, DIHLÍ.

THE LAT, OR STONE PILLAR OF FIRÚZ SHÁH, DIHLÍ.

CANTO II.

27

Fair gardens were there once—to ruin gone,
And silence in the Audience Chambers dwells,
The Pearl Mosque stands all sad, and still, and lone,
The Harím's echo of desertion tells,
O'er the proud turrets England's banner waves,
Her sentries pace the Halls with measured tread,
Not Halls of pleasure now, but pleasure's graves,
A Palace still, but Palace of the dead,
A form of beauty, but the life, the spirit, fled.

28

And this is modern Delhi—South a mile
Go view what was the city of Fírúz.
The Golden Pillar on its ruined pile
Looks o'er that city, now a bank of ooze.
Two thousand years have circled since the day
Asoka graved with laws that column fair
In Srughna; Fírúz brought it thence away,
And fixed the burden huge upstanding there,
To show, perhaps, where Indraprasthas limits were.

29

That city, too, is gone, long ages past,
But still some ruins, lingering on the site,
Lofty and lone, their warning shadows cast,
As if to show all glory has its night.
Southward of these upsprings Humáyún's tomb,
A Mausoleum vast, magnificent,
Methinks it needed not that lofty dome,
Nor those great sums in useless labour spent,
To keep alive a name with Akbar's glory blent.

THE KUTB MINÁR, DIHLÍ.

CANTO II.

30

Turn rather to that neighbouring, hallowed spot,
Where sleeps, beside a Saint, a saintly maid;
She lies as though oblivion were her lot,
His dust beneath rich canopies is laid.
She was of Tímúr's line, a princess, who
Resigned a Court to soothe a prisoned sire,
She did what Christians are required to do;
Her life was Love, made pure by Heaven's own fire,
That Love wherein all thoughts of earth and self expire.

31

A solitary slab her name imparts,
Upon the Sanctuary's extremest bound,
With simple words which sure must touch all hearts,
In which one spark of sympathy is found.
" Nor marble roof, nor gilded canopies,
O'er poor Jahánárá's last couch be spread;
The grass low bending to the gentle breeze
Is the best covering for her lowly bed;
'Twas Chishtí taught her, and to Heaven her footsteps led."

32

Still south of this, the Seven Castles rise,
But time would fail to tell of their extent,
Or of the Kutub's grace and giant size,
Heaven-kissing pillar, and world's ornament!
Or of the fort of Tughlak, or his tomb.
Not there, not 'mid the shadows of the past,
Among fall'n ruins and sepulchral gloom,
For this new Empire, fated long to last,
Should be, on this High day, the first foundations cast.

THE KUTB MINAR, DIHLÍ.
(Showing the Carving on the First Gallery.)

CANTO II.

33

Of better omen are the tracts that lie
Miles from those ruins to the far north-west,
For there has dawned the star of victory,
And there the light of Empire now shall rest.
There our avenging army halted long,
And there across the Ridge it fought its way,
Thence came the aid, at length, that made it strong,
And there the Rebels saw their strength decay,
As band by band they fell on many a bloody day.

34

In that auspicious quarter, then, were placed
North-west of Delhi, from the Kashmír gate
A league and demi-league, Pavilions graced
With all to please the eye, or fancy sate.
Not since the moment when in Shúshan's Hall
Six score and seven princes, each a king
In his own province, answered to the call
Of Xerxes, was such royal gathering,
As England's hour of triumph to those towers shall bring.

35

Like a fair bride arose the New Year's morn,
Not hid in clouds, as in the gloomy West,
Not of her smiles, or radiant tresses shorn,
But as a Queen in gold and amber dressed.
With roseate blush, on azure chariot borne,
The gems of heaven sparkling on her breast,
Scattering those hues that Paradise adorn,
Evangelist of good, she came most blest,
For nations to all time her glory shall attest.

Nº 1.
GENERAL VIEW OF THE GREAT DARBÁR AT DIHLÍ, 1ST JANUARY, 1877.

Nº 2.
GENERAL VIEW OF THE GREAT DARBÁR AT DIHLÍ, 1ST JANUARY, 1877.

CANTO II.

36

And on her rising, forth from Delhi pour
Streams upon streams, a sea of human life,
Not, as when erst the Northern champions bore
Aid to our cause, to meet us in fierce strife,
But to clasp hands, past troubles to forget,
To silence malice, strike dissension dumb,—
Well! their goodwill with goodwill shall be met,
Heed not those pealing cannons and that drum;
Their message is not war, they tell that peace is come.

37

It was a vast and strangely mingled throng
That to the Hall of Empire hastened then;
There, trampling on, the moving mass among,
Rode many a Chieftain with his armed men;
And there in loftier state, bedecked, begemmed,
On his huge elephant each Prince was seen;
Scarce the great beast the living torrent stemmed,
But with slow swinging step the ranks between
Picked cautiously its way, or wounds and death had been.

38

There in their curtained Raths [17] passed on the fair,
And coyly moved at times the obstructive veil,
But quickly shunned the gazer's ill-bred stare,
Nor would his glances with their charms regale;
There the fat Banyá in his ox-drawn car,
Sleek as the oil he sells, paced slowly on;
There startled camels progress strove to bar,
With necks aloft the passage seemed to con,
Then, stung with idle fears, they pushed their way along.

CANTO II.

39

At length the Halls were reached, the march was done,
An Indian crowd shouts never its applause,
The brightest spectacle beneath the sun
From them at most a murmured plaudit draws.
But then they showed some signs of pleased surprise,
As they beheld a temple fit to hold
An Empress when fair France with England vies
In splendour at some field of cloth of gold,
And saw the dazzling Halls that did that tower enfold.

40

The Halls were crescent shaped, the temple high,
And in the midst it stood, so all that sate
In the pavilions could with ease descry
That central Dais and its throne of State.
As yet 'twas empty, but not so the Halls,
For India's Princes fast were gathering there,
Each had his seat assigned within the walls
Of the most northern, and around his chair
His champions stood, each chief might India's standard bear.

41

For they were noble, noble as the knights
That sat King Arthur's table once around.
There have of old I trow been glorious sights,
And chivalry has oft bright welcomes found,
And ancient Persia's feasts with jewels shone,
And Roman triumphs brilliant scenes displayed,
But ne'er did eye of mortal look upon
A scene more dazzling than was there surveyed;
All India's wealth and glory in one spot arrayed.

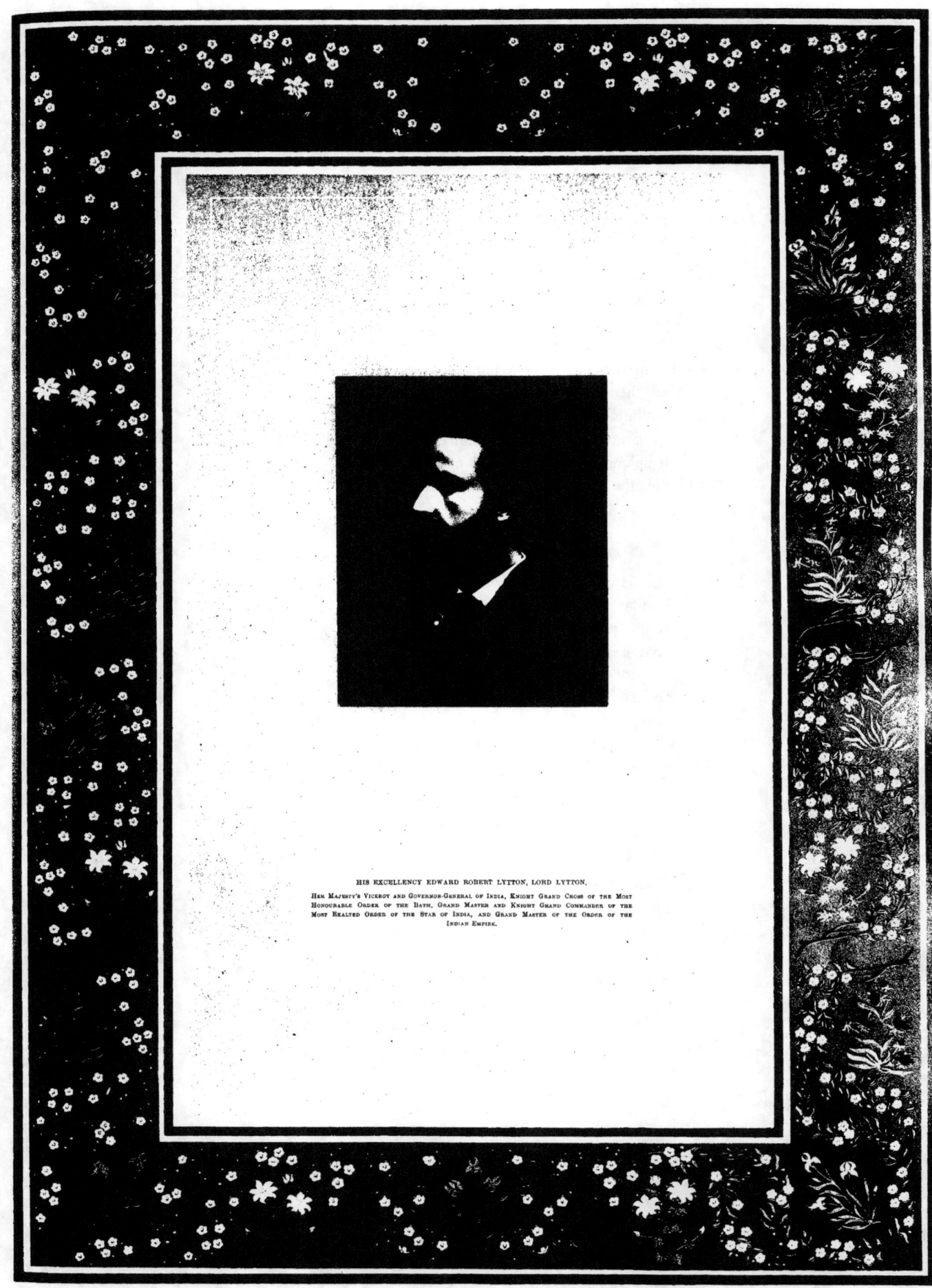

HIS EXCELLENCY EDWARD ROBERT LYTTON, LORD LYTTON,

Her Majesty's Viceroy and Governor-General of India, Knight Grand Cross of the Most Honourable Order of the Bath, Grand Master and Knight Grand Commander of the Most Exalted Order of the Star of India, and Grand Master of the Order of the Indian Empire.

CANTO II.

42

North of this Hall a thousand elephants
In two-fold line a double barrier made,
Boast not thyself, O man! 'tis Heaven that grants
Thy reason by Titanic force obeyed.
South of the central tower two Halls were filled
With thrice a thousand gazers from all lands,
With bevies of fair women, whose hearts thrilled
With eager wish to hear their Queen's commands.
Around a crowd was gathered countless as the sands.

43

Westward two hosts, as far as eye could reach,
Filled up the plain, which glittered, as at night
The white surf glitters breaking on the beach,
So sparkled there their weapons steely light.
One host was English, that their movement just,
Light but firm step, and dauntless bearing told.
The other, too, was worthy of all trust,
Though English not in name, it too was bold
And loyal, one in spirit, by one will controlled.

44

Now all was hushed and expectation stirred
Men's hearts, until the silver trumpets blew
A stirring blast, then swiftly passed the word,
And swords leapt out, and flags and pennons flew,
And gay with waving plumes and flashing arms
A gallant squadron came, swift dashing by,
'Mid which one might espy, too, women's charms,
And on the cortége sped right royally,
And at the Dais halting, took their seats on high.

THE RIGHT HONOURABLE EDITH, LADY LYTTON, C.I.
(i.e. (A Lady of the Imperial Order of the Crown of India.))

CANTO II.

45

And who was worthy there to fill that day
The throne of Empire in his sovereign's stead?
Who but the Poet-Statesman, born to sway
Senates, and the tide of thought to lead.
One who is firm to make the strong obey,
Repress the violent and humble pride,
But kind—the brilliant, cautious, thoughtful, gay.
Lytton! who e'er before so well allied
The art to govern men with art that art to hide.

46

And in his footsteps graceful trod one who,
Say not she might be, is in look a queen,
As fair as Arthur's, but more wise and true;
Slender and tall as lilies—well I ween,
For such bright eyes that knights would battle do
With kings, aye, would with gods,—of noblest birth,
Yet meek and gentle and devoted too.
Such beauty is, I trow, most rare on earth,
Of beauty gemmed with virtues thus is greater dearth.

47

Nor was there wanting England's noblest there,[18]
For there sat one whose great progenitress
Was Queen of France. Her grandchild, born to wear
The Crown of England, from it borrowed less
Of lustre than in beauty's light arrayed
Her innocence bestowed upon it—well!
'Twas, or 'twas not her right—but she obeyed
Her Sire's behest, and so a martyr fell,
And long shall sorrowing tongues her piteous story tell!

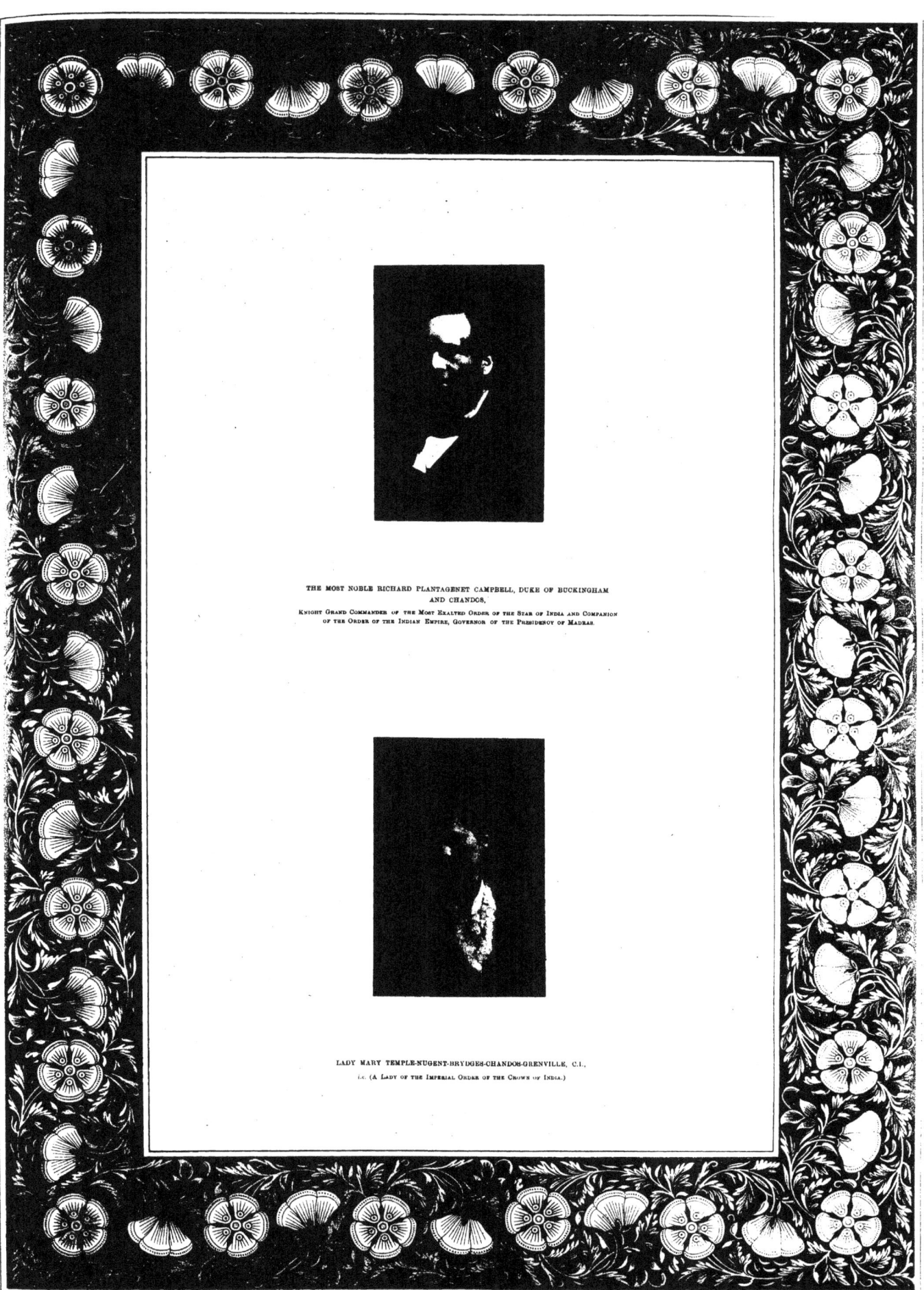

CANTO II.

48

And now the High Assemblage was complete,
The heralds ready stood, the throne was filled,
Each prince's flag waved o'er him in his seat,
All hearts with pleasure and expectance thrilled.
But say, O Muse, amid that princely throng,
Who in that sparkling crescent faced the throne,
To whom the poet's praises first belong?
Whose presence first his tuneful strain should own?
Whose titles to the world his song should first make known.

49

Of England's firm Ally, then, first I sing,
Who in the centre of that glittering line
Attentive sat—himself a youthful king,
In whose fair lot all fortune's gifts combine.
Wider his realm than Greece or Italy,
And loyal subjects his mild rule obey,
What foe shall come his peaceful frontier nigh,
So long as England's Empress-Queen bears sway!
First through her sheltering lands such foe must force his way.

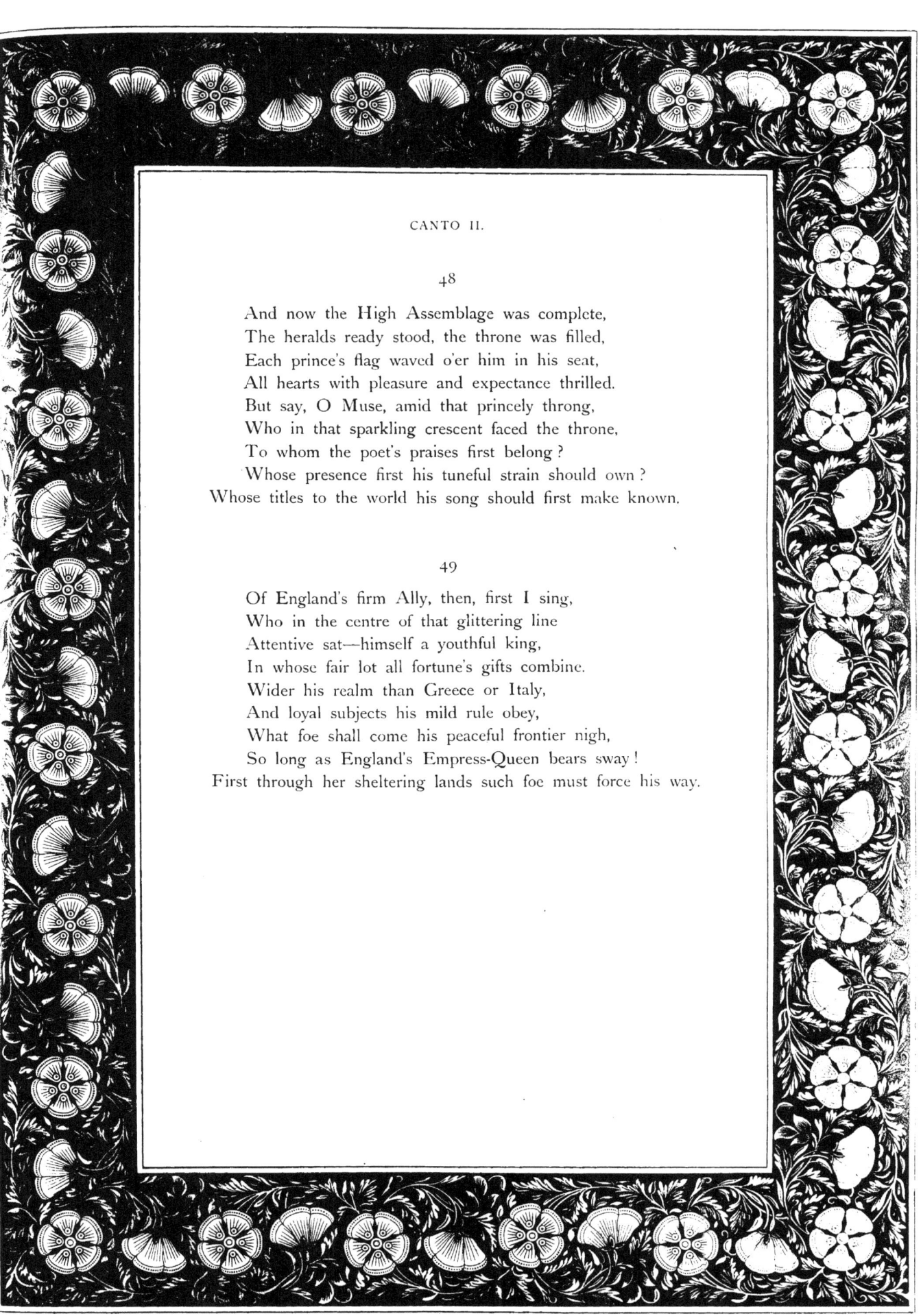

SIR PHILIP EDMOND WODEHOUSE,
Knight Grand Commander of the Most Exalted Order of the Star of India, and Knight Commander of the Most Honourable Order of the Bath, late Governor of the Presidency of Bombay.

CANTO III.

THE NIZAM OF THE DAKHAN.

1

From the second Khalíf [19] sprung,
    From Sohwardi's sacred line,
    Saint and sage of gifts divine,
On whose teaching mankind hung,
    Lifted from their state supine,
Thou Nizám shalt first be sung,
    India's potentates among.
For thee frail Fortune shall her wheel resign,
And change her fickle nature to rest wholly thine.

2

Of the noble noblest thou!
    Kings and saints thy ancestry
    Names bequeathed that ne'er shall die;
Names that gild thy scutcheon now.
    May thy glory with their's vie!
Fate heard thy forefather's vow,
    Gave him lands and wealth enow;
Blest the ascetic's loaf [20] with victory,
And in his banner set the hallowed sign on high.

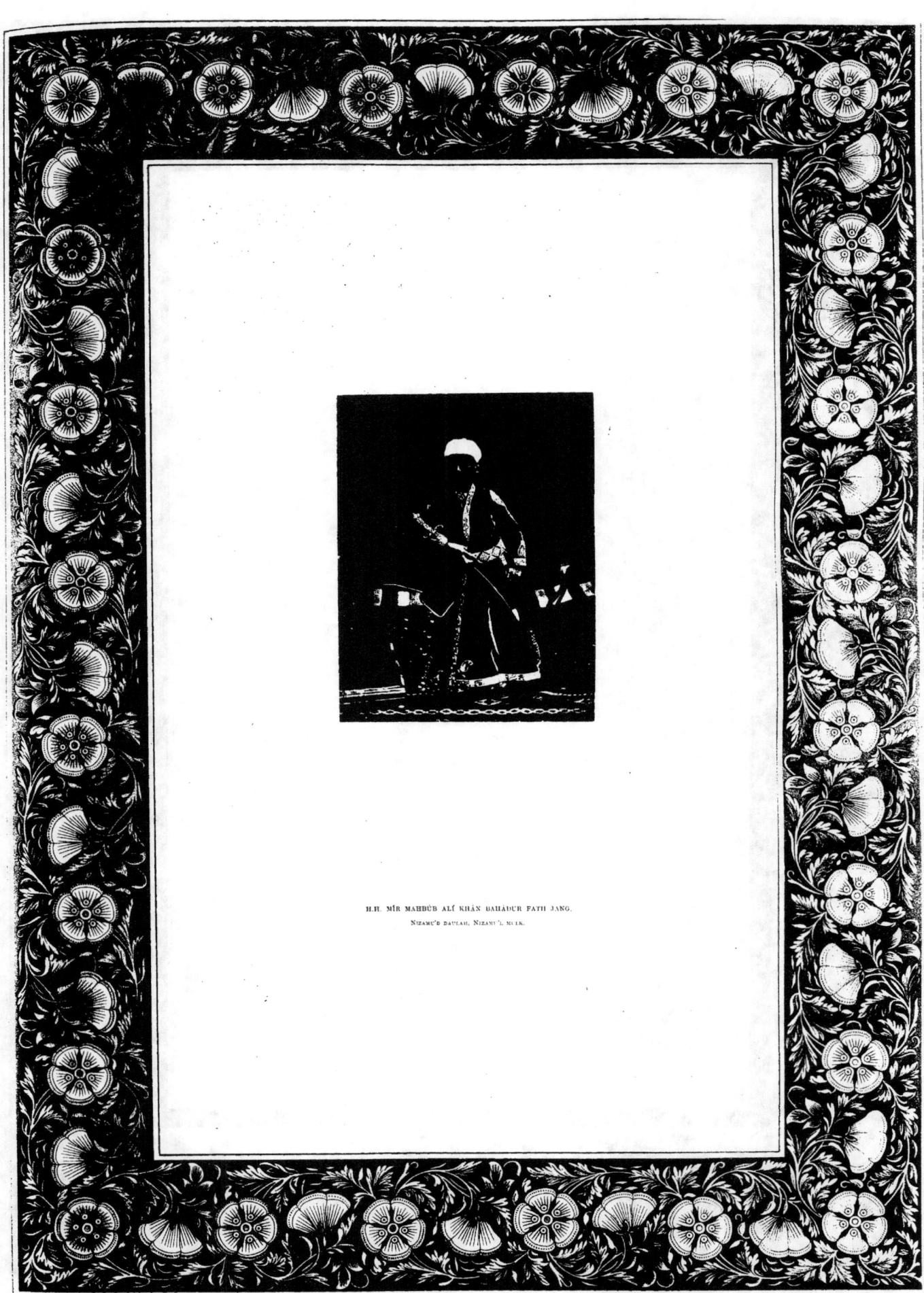

H.H. MÍR MAHBÚB ALÍ KHÁN BAHÁDUR FATH JANG.
Nizámu'd daulah, Nizámu'l mulk.

CANTO III.

3

India then was riven in twain,
    Severed like to warp from weft,
    Half to Delhi's king was left;
But the Mughul strove in vain,[21]
    Of the southern half bereft,
His proud 'vantage to retain,
Empire lost to win again.
Fate had that empire vast asunder cleft,
And from the Imperial crown its brightest jewel reft.

4

All men dream of rank and power,
    Dream 'tis bliss to be a king,
    And such dreams illusions bring.
Lengthening out life's tiny hour,
    O'er it they enchantment fling;
Courts they deck with many a flower,
Culled from Fancy's fairy bower.
But ah! to care for millions is a thing,
That with a million cares, methinks, the heart must wring.

5

If 'tis thus, then royal child!
    'Twas the blessing of thy birth,
    More than gold, than rubies worth,
'Twas that Heaven propitious smiled,
    That it with thy share of earth,
Gave thee one, who tamed the wild,[22]
And the wayward reconciled,
A regent, who has changed distress to mirth,
And spread abundance, where before were want and dearth.

The Armorial Bearings
of
His Highness the Nizam

CANTO III.

6

From Medína's sacred walls,
    Came his noble Arab sire.[23]
    Suns shall set, long years expire,
Ere oblivion's mantle falls
    On that advent, or men tire,
Of a memory, that recalls
    Vijyapura's once bright halls,
Blended with names that noblest thoughts inspire,
Names in whose praise bards shall for ages tune the lyre.

7

Of those names I sing but one,
    One the Dakhan knows full well,
    Long shall Southern India tell
Good deeds by Sir Sálár done.
    Monks may hope in gloomy cell
Heaven by prayer and fasts is won,
    By the men who mankind shun.
But better they who can their passions quell,
Live in, not of, the world, heaven-gazing vanquish Hell.

8

Young King of the Dakhan—Yes!
    All too tender are thy years
    To assuage a nation's fears,
Or their aspirations bless.
    Thou a Pilot need'st, who steers
Calm in danger and distress,
    For thy people's happiness.
A Guide who with his own thy name endears,
And for thy coming reign a stately fabric rears.

H.E. THE NŪWAB MUKHTARU'D DAULAH, SIR SALAR JANG BAHADUR, G.C.S.I.,
Regent of the Nizam's Dominions.

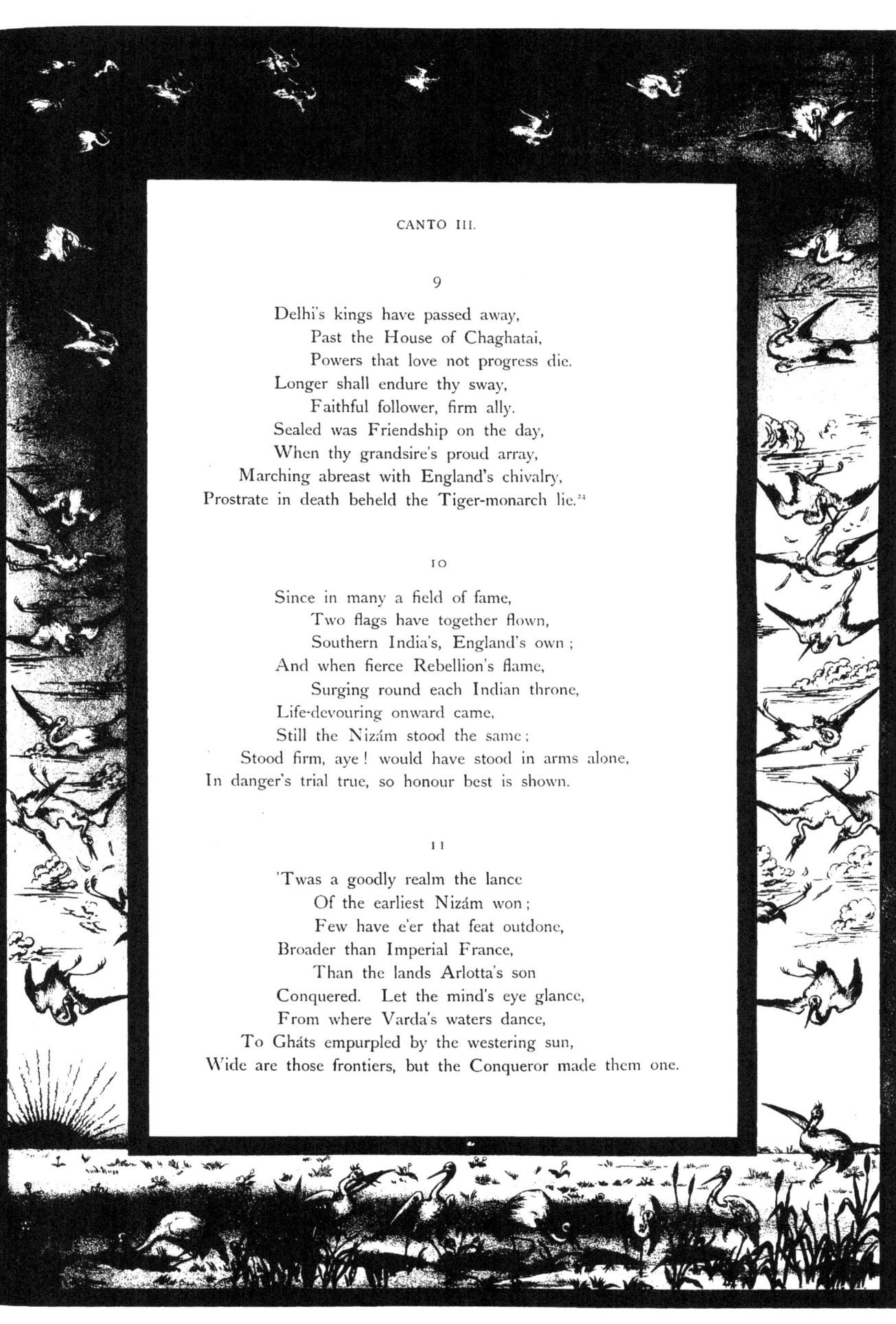

CANTO III.

9

Delhi's kings have passed away,
    Past the House of Chaghatai,
    Powers that love not progress die.
Longer shall endure thy sway,
    Faithful follower, firm ally.
Sealed was Friendship on the day,
    When thy grandsire's proud array,
Marching abreast with England's chivalry,
Prostrate in death beheld the Tiger-monarch lie.[24]

10

Since in many a field of fame,
    Two flags have together flown,
    Southern India's, England's own;
And when fierce Rebellion's flame,
    Surging round each Indian throne,
Life-devouring onward came,
    Still the Nizám stood the same;
Stood firm, aye! would have stood in arms alone,
In danger's trial true, so honour best is shown.

11

'Twas a goodly realm the lance
    Of the earliest Nizám won;
    Few have e'er that feat outdone,
Broader than Imperial France,
    Than the lands Arlotta's son
Conquered. Let the mind's eye glance,
    From where Varda's waters dance,
To Gháts empurpled by the westering sun,
Wide are those frontiers, but the Conqueror made them one.

SIR SÁLÁR JANG'S PALACE.

PALACE OF THE NIZÁM, HAIDARÁBÁD.

SIR SÁLÁR JANG'S PALACE.

PALACE OF THE NIZÁM, HAIDARÁBÁD.

CANTO III.

12

Belted round with stony bands,
   But in robes of verdure drest,
   And with sparkling waters blest,
Haidar's giant City stands,
   Second city of the west.
Well that capital commands
All the Dakhan's wide-spread lands,
Long have the sons of Islám there found rest.
Nor has their fortress e'er a foeman's rule confest.

13

Stronger still, in lonely pride,
   Frowns the rock-hewn citadel,
   Where, as ancient stories tell,
With a nation at his side,
   Delhi's monarch strove to dwell:
Vainly, for back ebbed the tide
Of life—So the fates deride
The impotence of man, and swift repel
That which they favour not, though he may like it well.

14

Yet not always Deogarh,[25]
   This the ancient name is, viewed
   From its heights a solitude.
Time was that the mighty stir
   Of a countless multitude
Rose beside it, and the whir
Of a myriad prayer-wheels, ere
Men were with Islám's doctrines yet imbued,
Or Isá's voice dispelled the ancient credence rude.

THE BRITISH RESIDENCY AT HAIDARÁBAD.

GOLKONDAH TOMBS.

CANTO III.

15

Fronting that rock-castle then
    On the neighbouring mountain side
      Stretched a city, like the bride
Of the savage Shiva, when
      She reclines in beauty's pride
Near the scourge of gods and men.
Famous was it—In the ken
Of old-world Greeks it flourished, who spread wide
Its name, and Tagara with tales of wealth allied.

16

Ruins show still where it lay,
    And upon the hilltop near,
      Lies one—once a name of fear—
Mightiest monarch of his day,
      Last great Mughul, Álamgír.
On that hillside stretch away
    Verul's temples—Who can say
Where are art-wonders that eclipse those here?
Not Greece can show their like, nor Egypt boasts their peer.

17

Day by day, and year by year,
    Artists many a myriad toiled,
      Naught their steady ardour foiled.
Labouring on through centuries drear,
      Wearied, cramped, fordone, bemoiled,
From the rock they hewed out sheer
    Stately shrines and cells austere.
Nor crouching panther feared, nor serpent coiled,
Hunger, nor thirst, nor heat, nor cold, their emprise spoiled.

GOLKONDAH FORT.

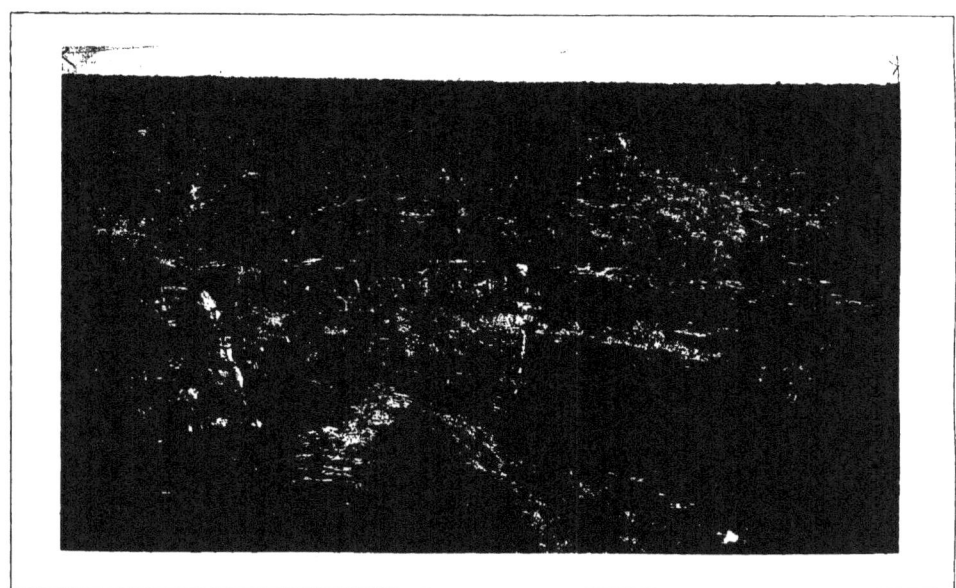

GENERAL VIEW OF THE CAVES OF AJANTA.

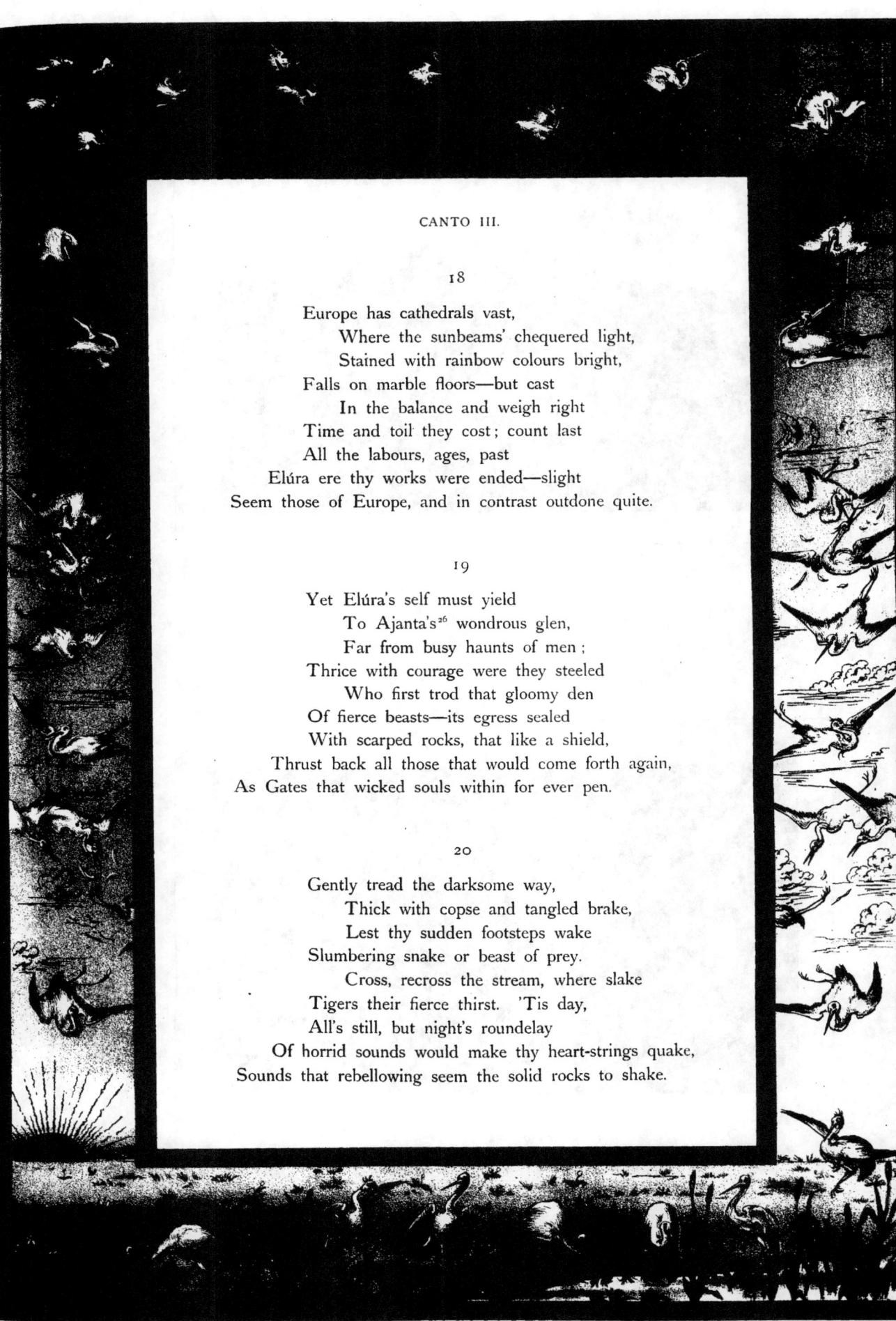

CANTO III.

18

Europe has cathedrals vast,
    Where the sunbeams' chequered light,
    Stained with rainbow colours bright,
Falls on marble floors—but cast
    In the balance and weigh right
Time and toil they cost; count last
All the labours, ages, past
Elúra ere thy works were ended—slight
Seem those of Europe, and in contrast outdone quite.

19

Yet Elúra's self must yield
    To Ajanta's[26] wondrous glen,
    Far from busy haunts of men;
Thrice with courage were they steeled
    Who first trod that gloomy den
Of fierce beasts—its egress sealed
With scarped rocks, that like a shield,
    Thrust back all those that would come forth again,
As Gates that wicked souls within for ever pen.

20

Gently tread the darksome way,
    Thick with copse and tangled brake,
    Lest thy sudden footsteps wake
Slumbering snake or beast of prey.
    Cross, recross the stream, where slake
Tigers their fierce thirst. 'Tis day,
All's still, but night's roundelay
    Of horrid sounds would make thy heart-strings quake,
Sounds that rebellowing seem the solid rocks to shake.

AJANTA.—FACADE OF VIHÂRA CAVE I, A.D. 500.

AJANTA.—VERANDAH OF CAVE I, A.D. 450.

GENERAL VIEW OF THE CAVES OF AJANTA.

AJANTA.—FRONT OF VIHÂRA CAVE II.

AJANTA.—VIHÂRA CAVE VII, A.D. 100 TO 200.

CANTO III.

21

Here, where ends the dark ravine,
    Look up and a marvel see,
    Work of sprites it well might be;
Cells and shrines that once have been
    Homes of many a votary,
Seam the rock's face—Well I ween
    Search the world through, such a scene
Exists not elsewhere, nor could fantasy
For man's devotion frame so strange a sanctuary.

22

There the Buddhist sought to tame
    All the passions of the soul,
    Sought extinction as his goal.
Nature thwarted bides the same,
    Tortured still escapes control;
To obey should be man's aim,
    None can dispensation claim
From Heaven's law. As magnets seek the Pole,
So man seeks life, and life eternal crowns his rôle.

23

Vainly then those hermits strove—
    But the narrow pathway climb,
    See all that neglect and time
Have bequeathed us. Cautious move
    On the thin ledge—It were crime
Not to heed here—Those who love
    Life tread warily above
A hundred feet of abyss; and the slime
Of ages makes the rock more slippery still with grime.

AJANTA.—FACADE OF CHAITYA CAVE IX, B.C. 100.

AJANTA.—INTERIOR OF CHAITYA CAVE X, B.C. 150—200.

AJANTA.—VERANDAH OF CAVE II, ABOUT A.D. 400.

AJANTA.—INTERIOR OF CHAITYA CAVE XIX.

AJANTA.—FACADE OF CAVE XIX.

CANTO III.

24

In a crescent stretch the caves,
  From the east to west they run,
  With the movement of the sun.
Westward, where the torrent raves
  There our heavy task is done.
'Tis a task that courage craves,
  For no fence the totterer saves;
Long is the circuit and the down-path one,
Strange how those holy men their wondrous work begun!

25

Many a portal carved is there,
  Rich with figures weird and quaint,
  Mocking fiend and musing saint.
But within are chambers rare,
  And not Guido's self could paint
Groups of female forms more fair,
  With soft eyes and golden hair,
Than here are limned. In sooth he knew restraint
Who gazed, and gazing kept his conscience without taint.

26

Flowers like those of Paradise,
  White, red, and ethereal blue,
  Deck the walls with dazzling hue.
Hidden 'tis from human eyes
  Who those wondrous tablets drew.
Mystery of mysteries,
  That may reason's self surprise.
Two thousand years have faded from the view,
But failed to teach mankind the art their fathers knew.

AJANTA.—FACADE OF CHAITYA CAVE XIX.

AJANTA.—PORTION OF THE FRONT OF VIHÂRA CAVE XX, A.D. 600.

AJANTA.—FRONT OF VIHÂRA CAVE XXIII, A.D. 500 (?)

AJANTA.—INTERIOR OF CHAITYA CAVE XXVI, A.D. 500—600

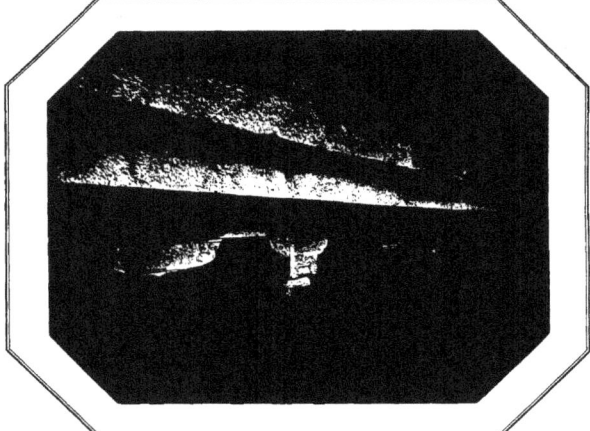
AJANTA.—FRONT OF VIHÂRA CAVE XXIV.

AJANTA.—FACADE OF CHAITYA CAVE XXVI, A.D. 400—500

CANTO III.

27

Other marvels might I sing,
    Dakhan! of thy glorious land;
    Thine the beautiful and grand,
Forest dense, and sparkling spring,
    Rivers over rock and sand
Rushing headlong down to bring
Tribute to their ocean king,
All that is fairest in fair Nature's hand
Is present and young prince! awaits thy high command.

28

Well might eyes towards thee turn,
    As in that Assembly High,
    First of Hind in dignity,
Thou sat'st; kingly though young. Stern
    Bosoms felt kind sympathy
For one who had yet to learn
Life; yet could they well discern
In thy bright features many a quality
Which dwelt in famous men, whose names will never die.

29

Fronting the Viceregal throne
    Thou wast then the cynosure
    Of all glances, but a pure
Disregard of self outshone
    From thy face ingenuous, sure
Of respect, but bent alone
Treasuring up to make thy own
Each word of that high message, and secure
That England's friendship so well won should long endure.

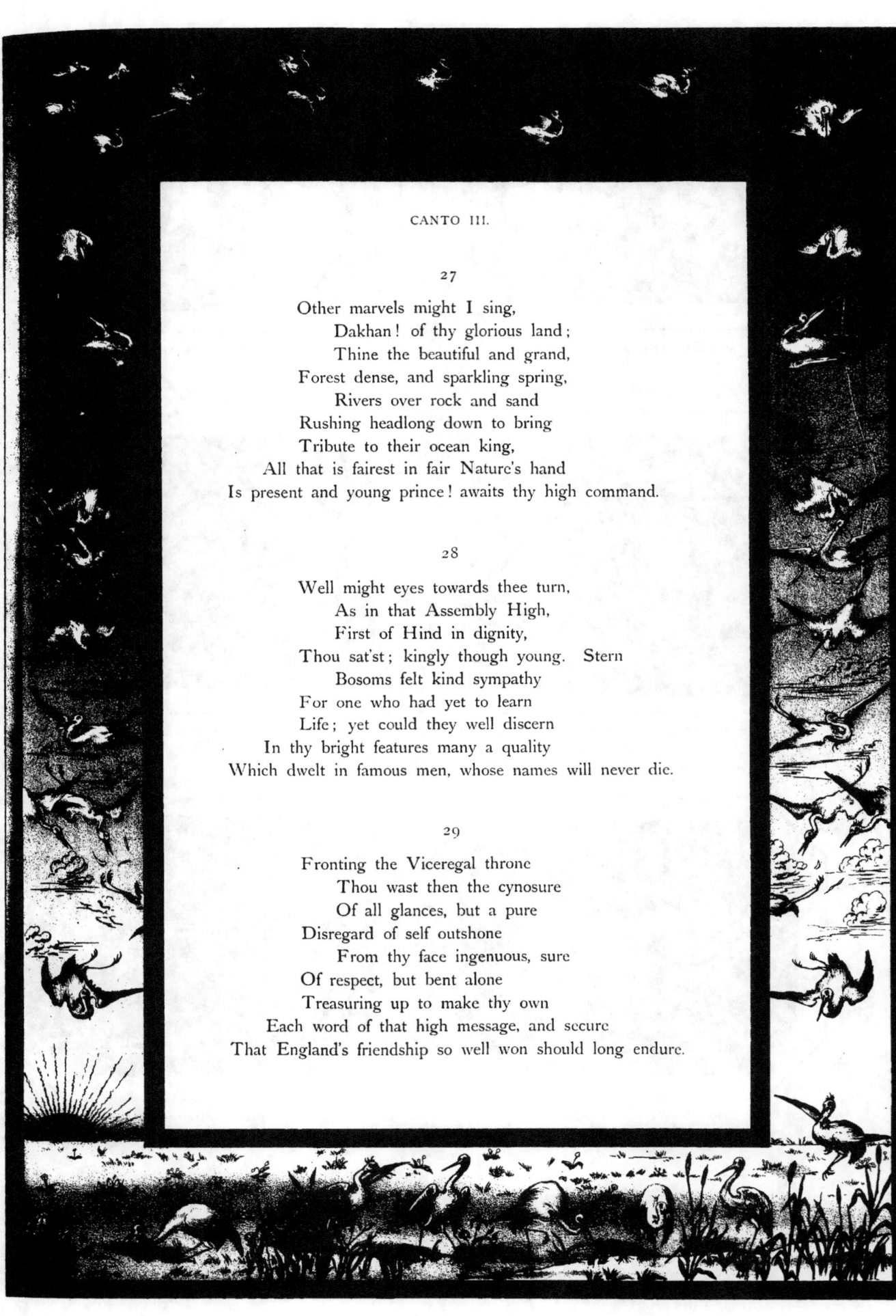

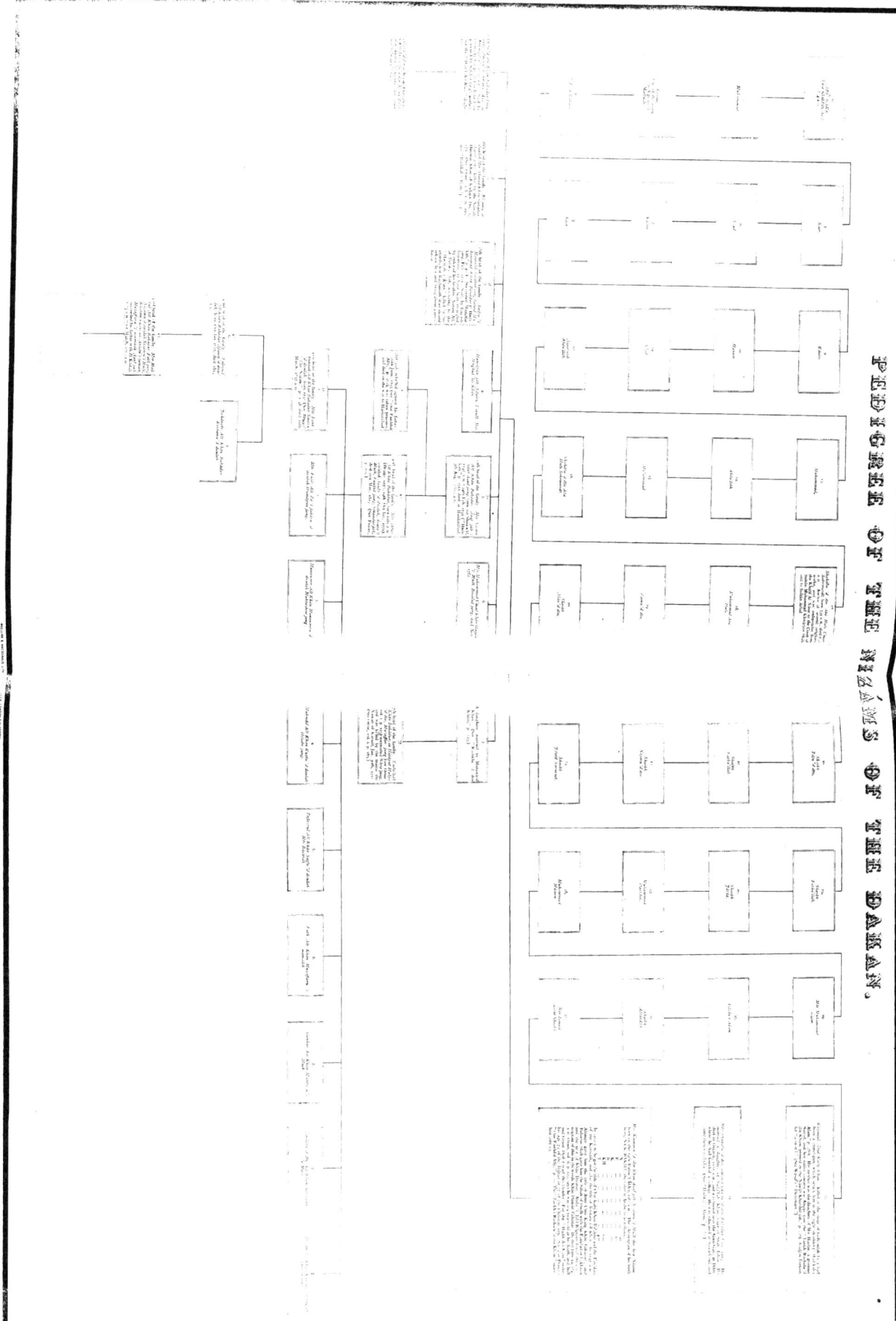

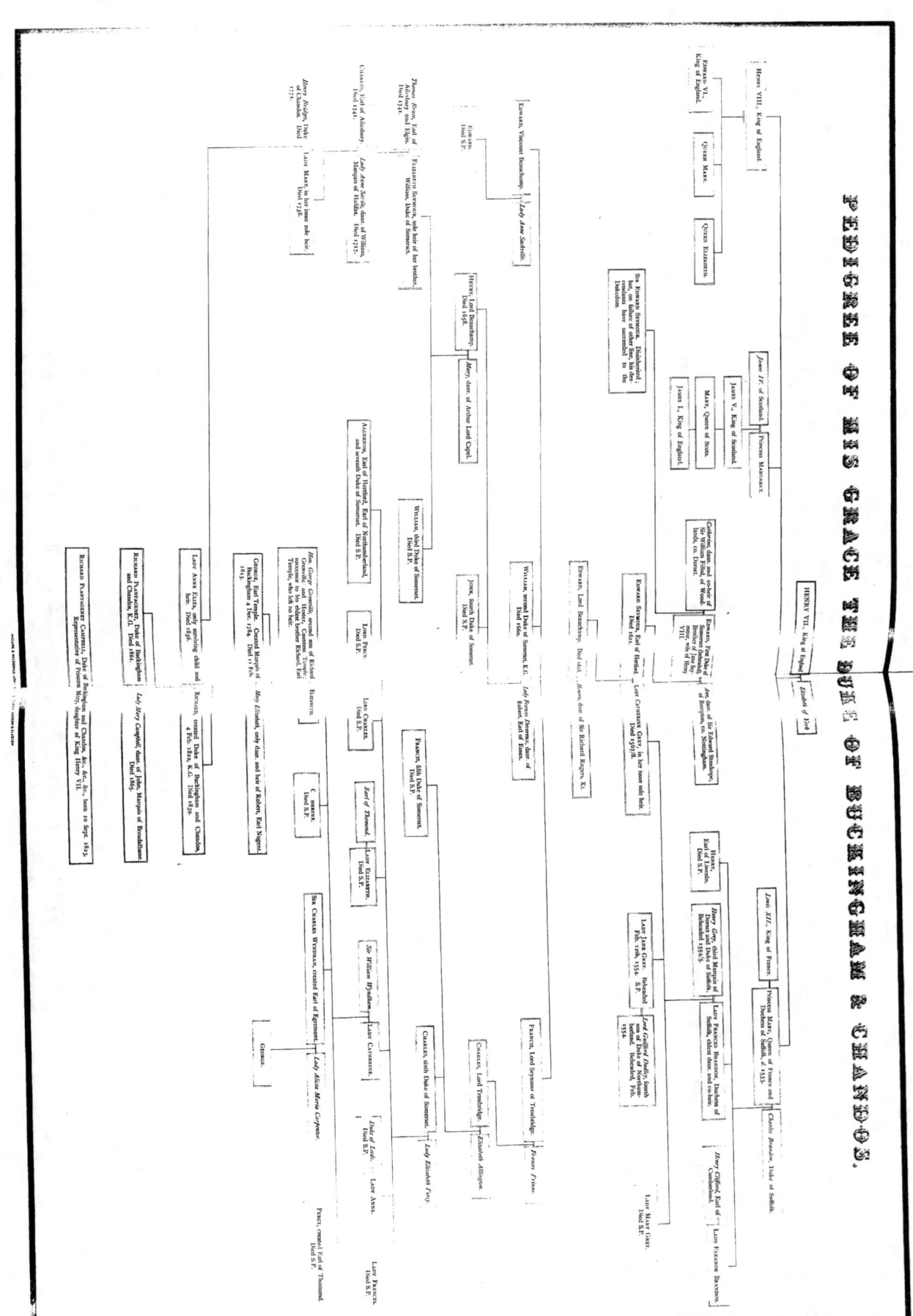

Canto 1. 1st Stanza

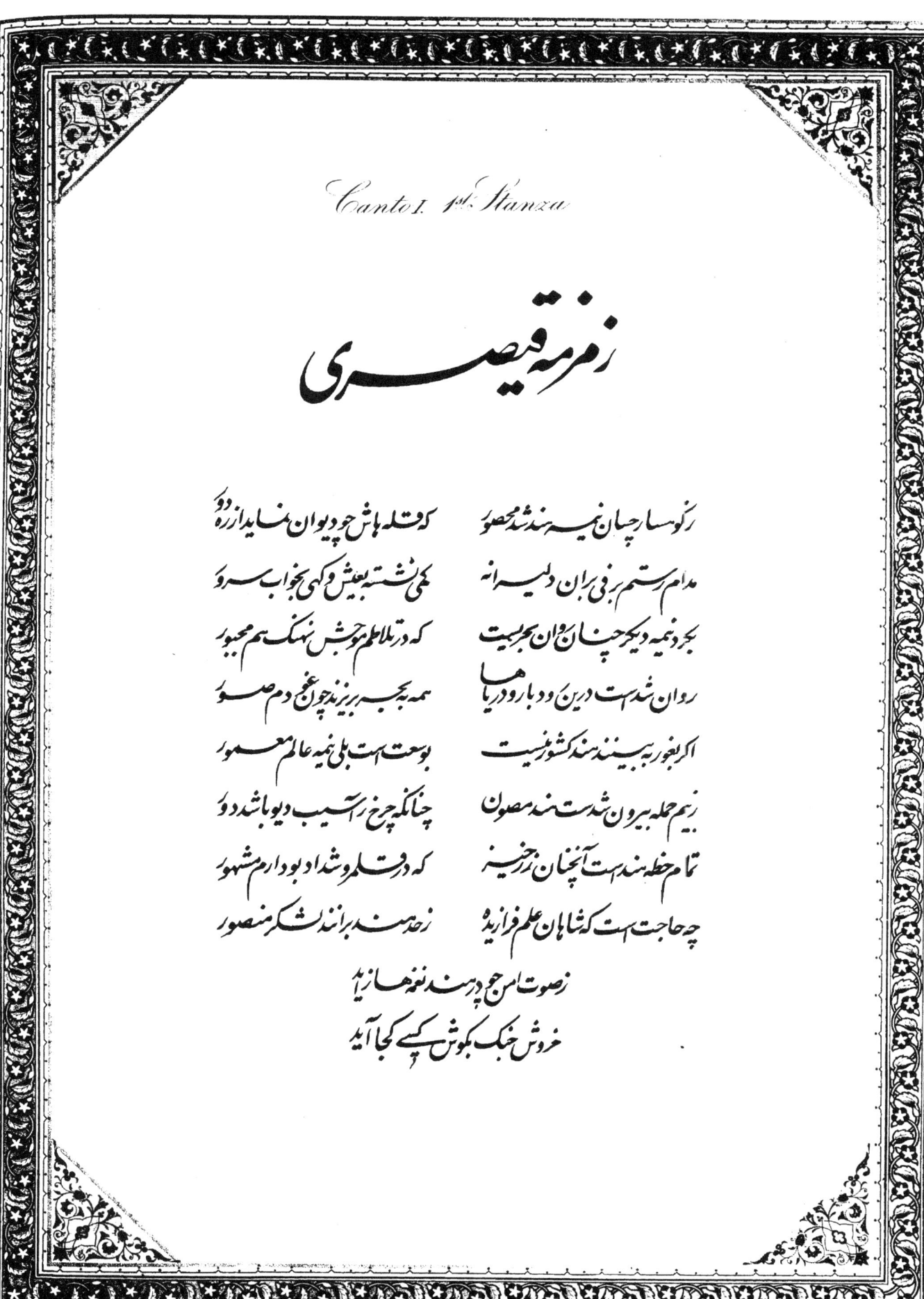

Canto 1 2nd & 3rd Stanzas

اگر وفاق بهندوستان علم بودی / و گر نهان بدل خلق مهر هم بودی

ز ترکتاز همه غم بر بیان سیمین تن / نواح دلکش این ملک بی الم بودی

و گر غنیم اولو العزم شورشی کردی / ز شور رستم و نیران و درزم بودی

چه کرد آمدی از سر دیار لشکر ها / که در شعاب جبالش خوش یم بودی

کز یخ تیز بجاش کر عدو آمدم / فکنده سر مه چون میش و چون غنم بودی

بنا کز یزدان دوست مرکزی ستشی
و کز نه راه اطاعت بجان و دل جستی

بمرغزار چنین ملک بوده آن در خو / که باغ مهربدی چون بهشت جنتم
دویده ریشه ی نفاق و کین سر جا / نهال انس این مرز خشک شد خسته
اگر چه هند بسی پر غم و خوشنما ملکست / ولیک ست در و مستبرد و وارد
بهو توبو تکل وادی است بلگفته / گیاه و برگ شجر بست سبز تر بکبیر
ثبوت کرده قدم را بشان مسعود ان / بواقعات و با سمار آریا کهنه
چه راز بود که در ابتدای خلق آنان / بیامدند بد ارفنا مثال شبه

هدایت همه شان جنگ ناصوابی شده
ملک هند خراب بی حسابی شده

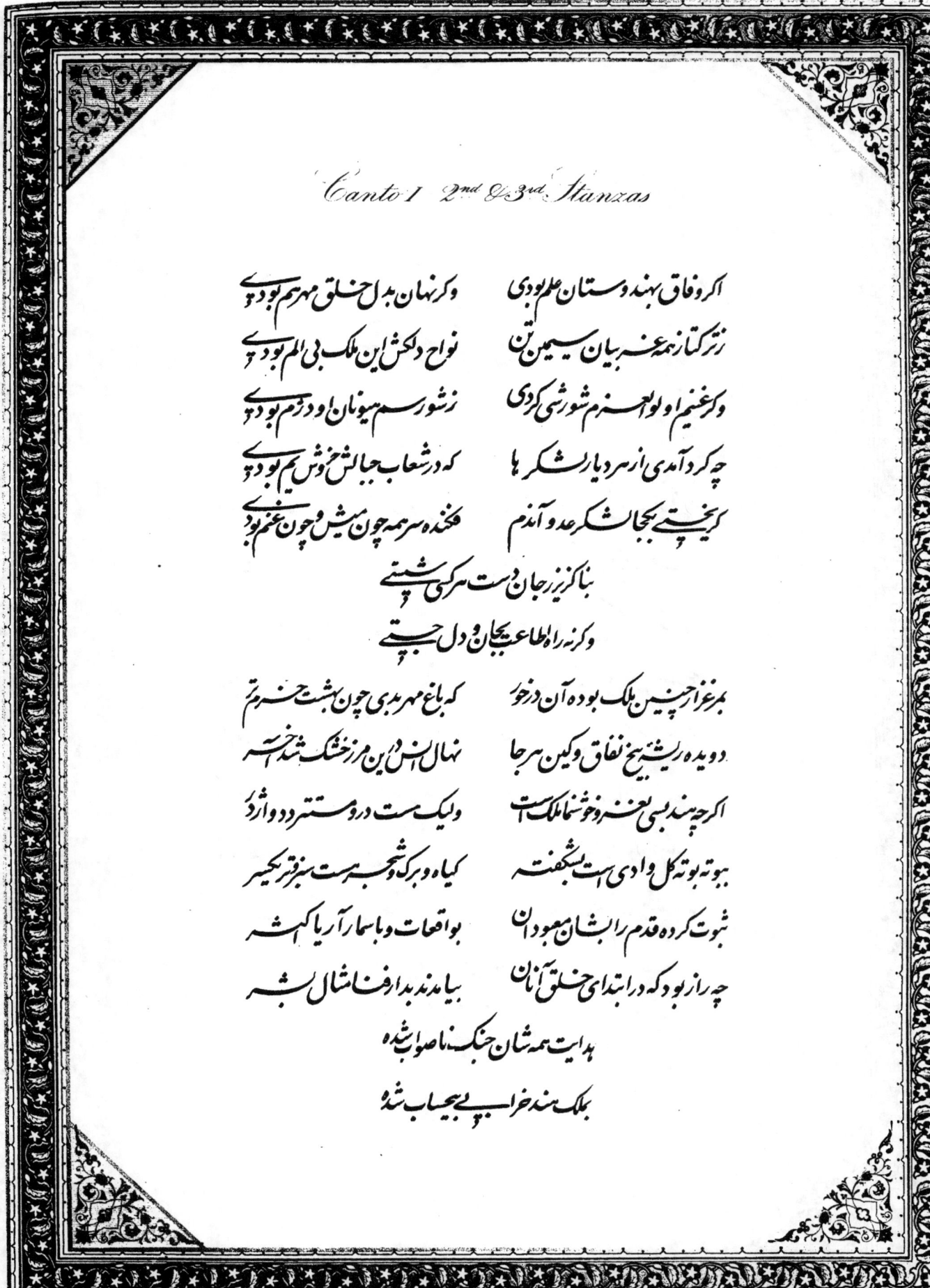

Canto 1. 4th & 5th Stanzas

باین نفاق بهندوستان چه گشت بود   که فوج حلگسان ازو نمیت بود
شنیده ایدا و الحضرمی سکندرا   ولی بهند نه آن همت و غیرت بود
ندیده چهره دلدار مدعا بر کشت   که کرد جان و دلش فوج یاس و حسرت بو
رسیده بود در قمت بچشمه حیوان   که آب صافیش در مغاک ظلمت بو
فرشته نیز نمی بت بر آن نه بال کشا   چه در جهات و نوعش حلال قدرت بو

شهیکه بخت رساند سر کجا او را
نمود فتح چنین ملک جان گزا او را

در آن مقام که با آن جنود خویش بیا   گزشته هست بستلج لبان خط غماس
تمام شکر اسکندری هما خبا ماند   قدم نهاد نه این دی بحجر کس نرس
ندای حبک پیاپی همی زد سکندر   بخرده کوش دلیری ابن کثرت ماس
ستاده بود چو دم ماند کان شیو نان   همی کشید دم ماذم ز سینه سرد انفاس
زجوش ما بین جان جز ین جز می گفت   که خواب با بین حال بدید کنج خلاف قیاس
برین وقایع چو کزشت سال و ملی سیا   بیامد ابر نبرد که بر د موش و حواس
تعجب هست که مردان هندرا انگاه   ز سول دل شده ناگاه طبع جن اکس

گریز کرده چو آن فوج در بیاس فتاد
تمام آب بیم از کثرت عریق استاد

Canto 1 6th & 7th Stanzas

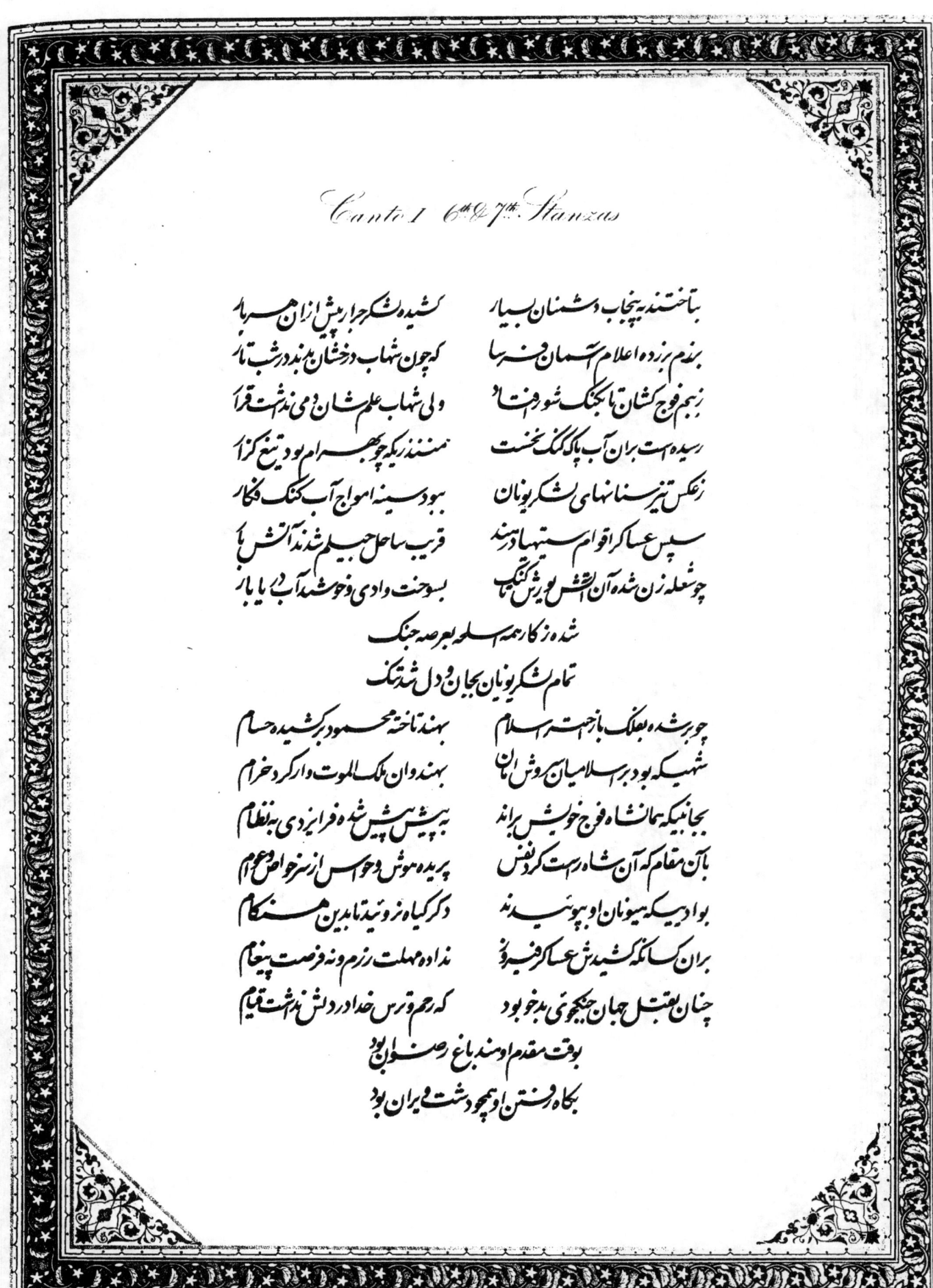

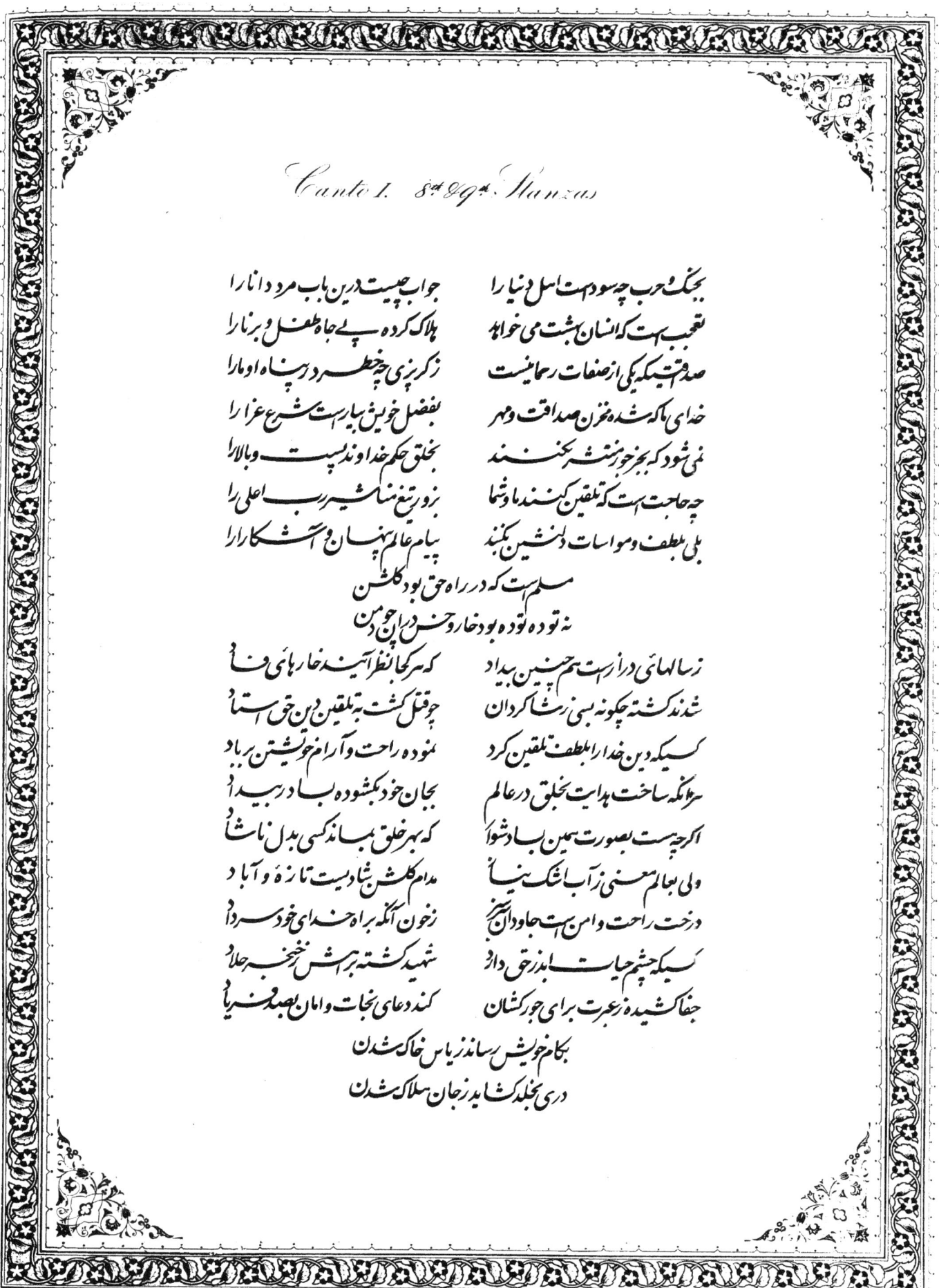

Canto I. 10th & 11th Stanzas

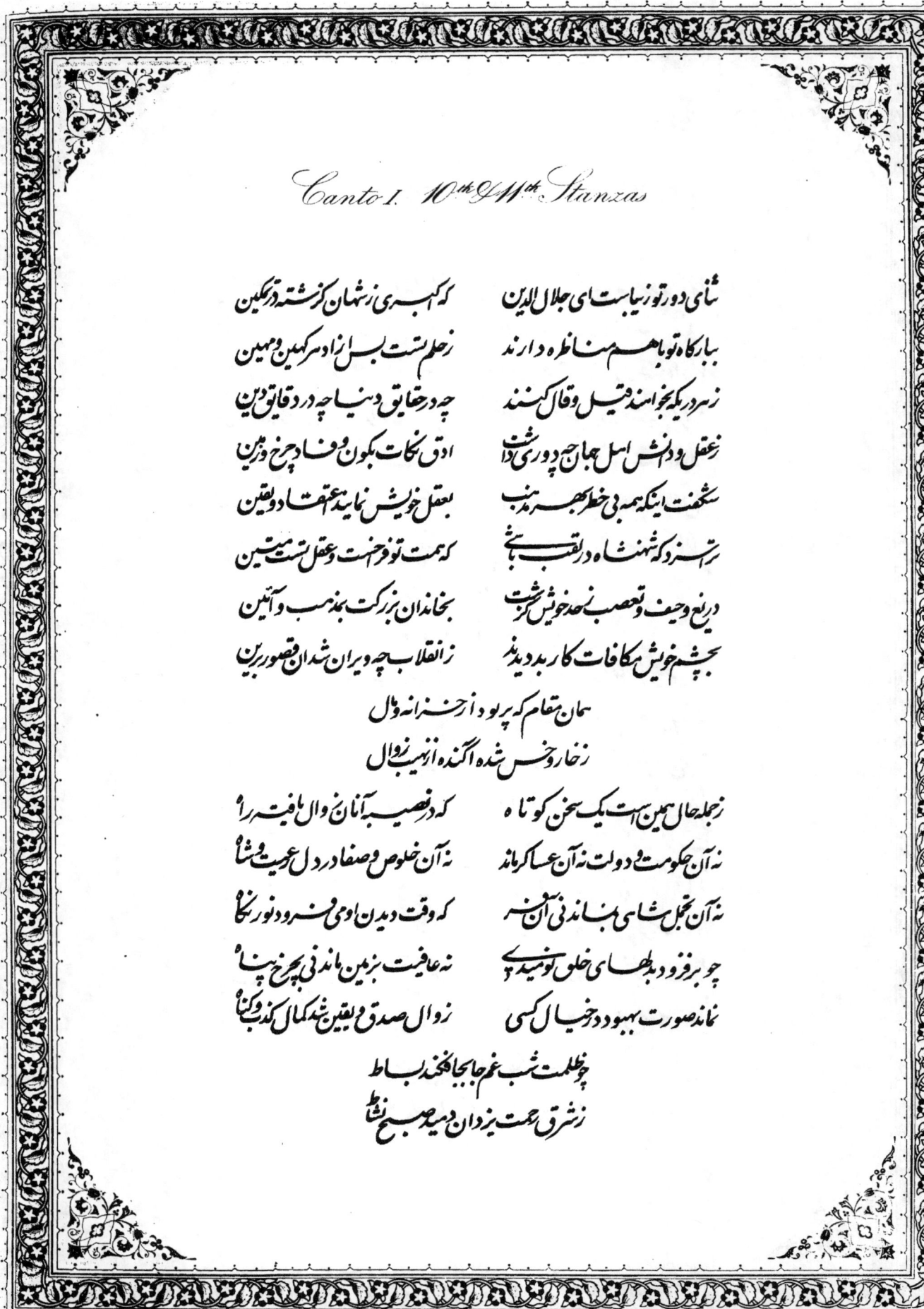

Canto I. 12th & 13th Stanzas

Canto I. 114th & 15th Stanzas

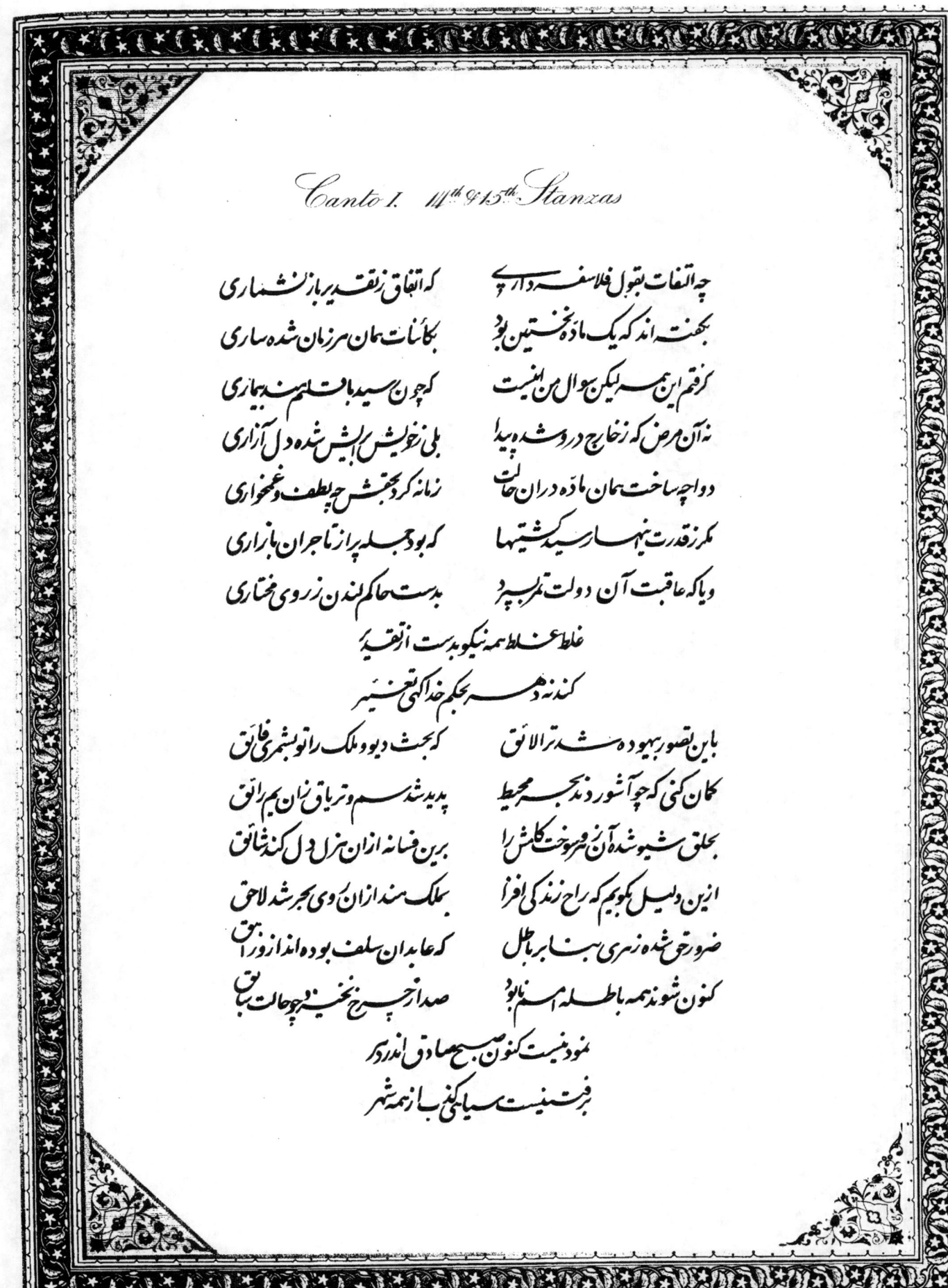

Canto 1. 16th & 17th Stanzas

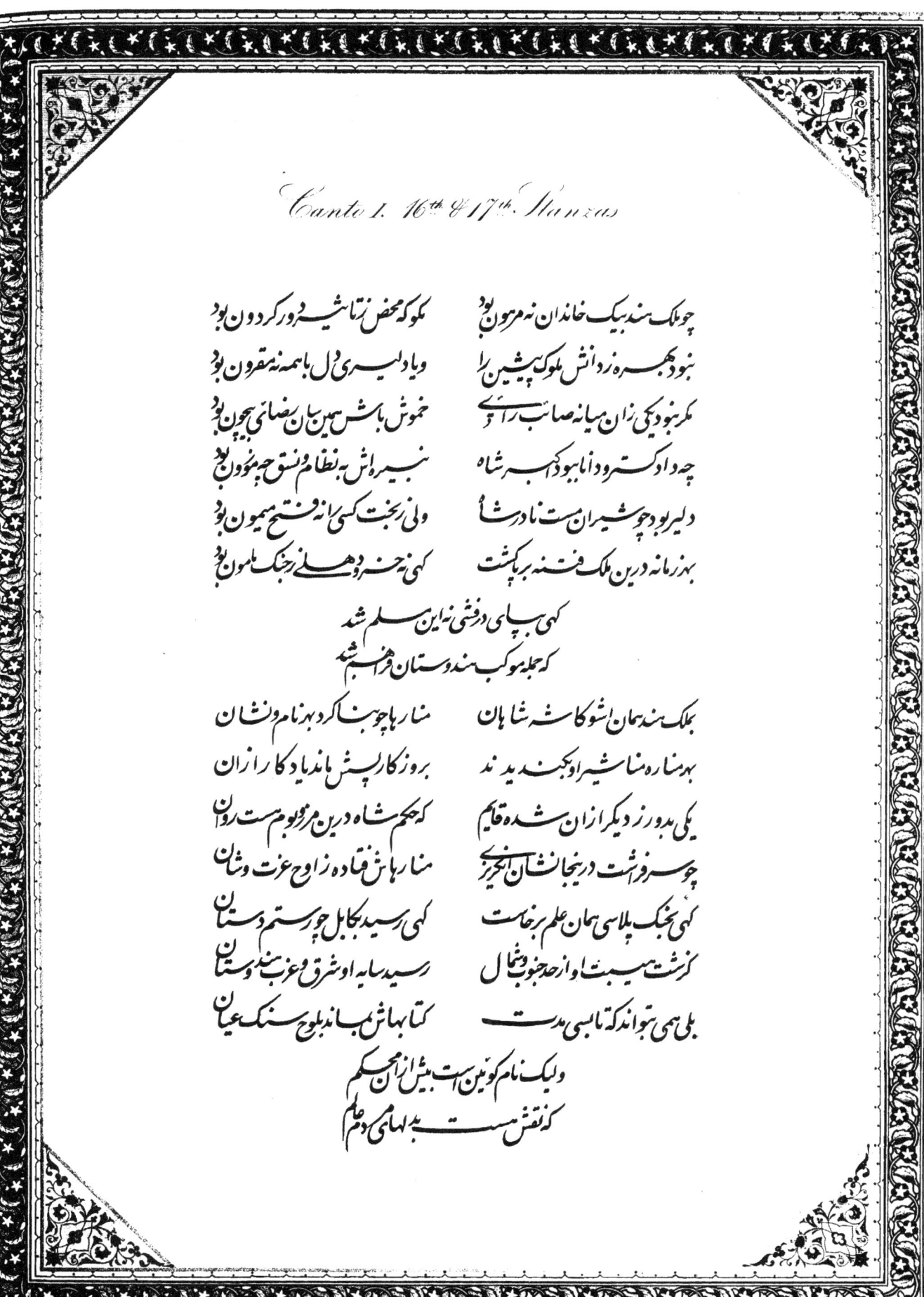

Canto I. 18th & 19th Stanzas

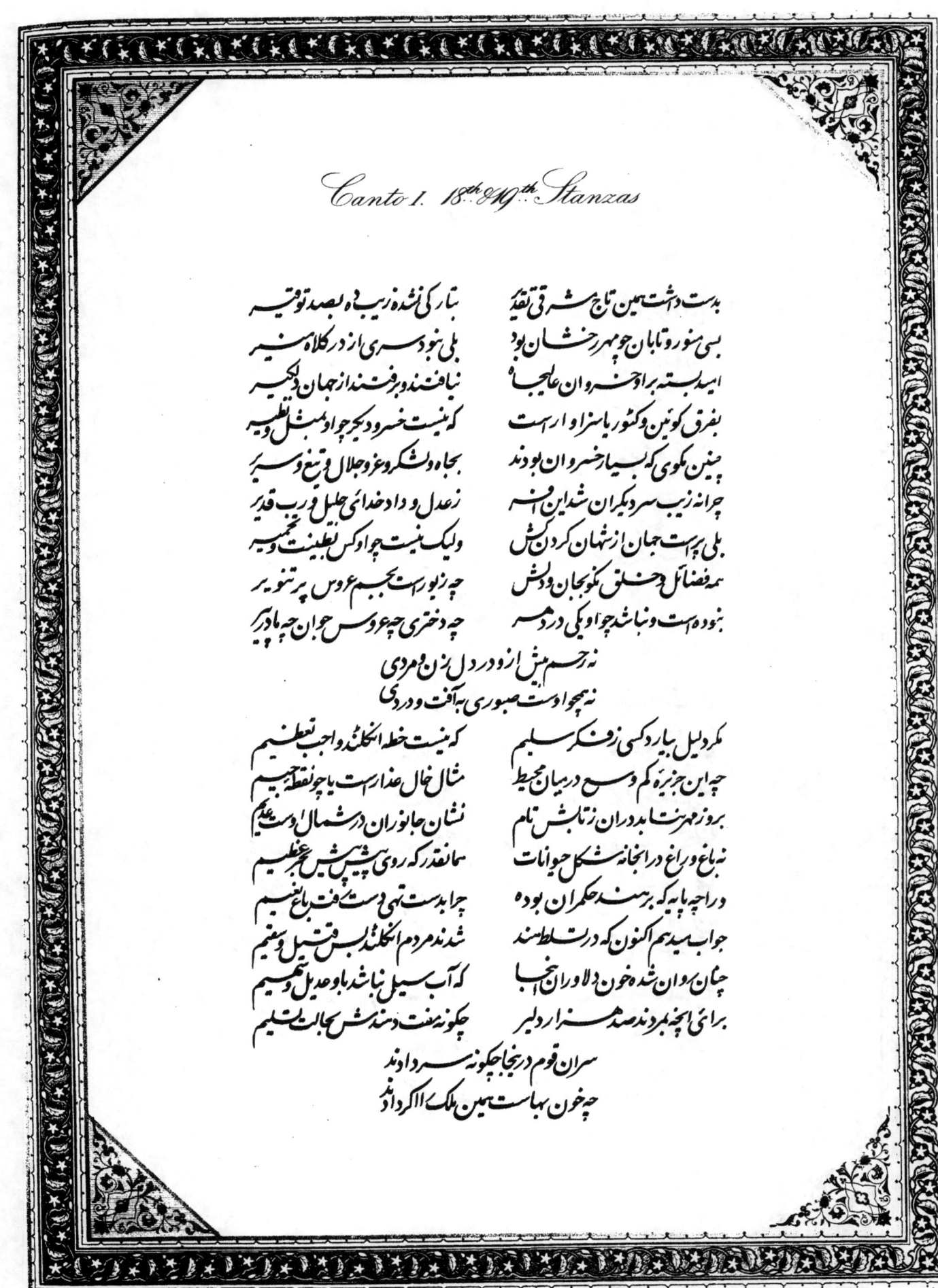

Canto 1. 20th & 21st Stanzas

خموش باش این باب کشتهٔ یکنیل   بدان که عزت و عظمت بود نجب جمیل

منو رہت چہ زنجیر جنگہای عظیم   که حلقهای طلایش نخرہ بند تفصیل

ازان فتوح که در سالها میبرند   بقالب آمده این سلسله زجد جریل

چگونه قوم بر ان افتخار نتوان کرد   چکونه مال بپس ما دکان بود سبیل

کسی که پیچ میکار دراین چنین عظمت   بلو که چون تن خاکی روان است نے لیل

کہی ور اسما کار نامه الکلنه   کہ این طرد نجیب است نی شخص ذیل

کسی که بیخرد و خوار شد چہ چیوانات

چہ اتفات بسویش کخن بطامات

چہ چیز بود که صد جان کنم برو برچے   شدند مردم سپارنا دلیر از روپے

بنو دیع دکرو اقعات آبود   کہ یادش آمد و دل جیش نفوج نشے

زنام تسمیر پولی دلیر کرد دل   کم جنگ بی مرد ست لغزه پے

کسی که قتل شد اینجا جنگ چہ میدان   ز آل او بدر آئینه نادیران کے

کسی که با جنہ تسرد راسائی و پہلے   کزہشتہ بیزان نخیلیش نادر شے

نہ زنہار بر آنان ہر کس چیرہ شود   بنام خویش نخواہند طعن بپی درچے

اکرچہ قوت فوج عدو بود دچند

کریز کرد چہ آب خاندان ریزند

Canto 1. 22ⁿᵈ & 23ʳᵈ Stanzas

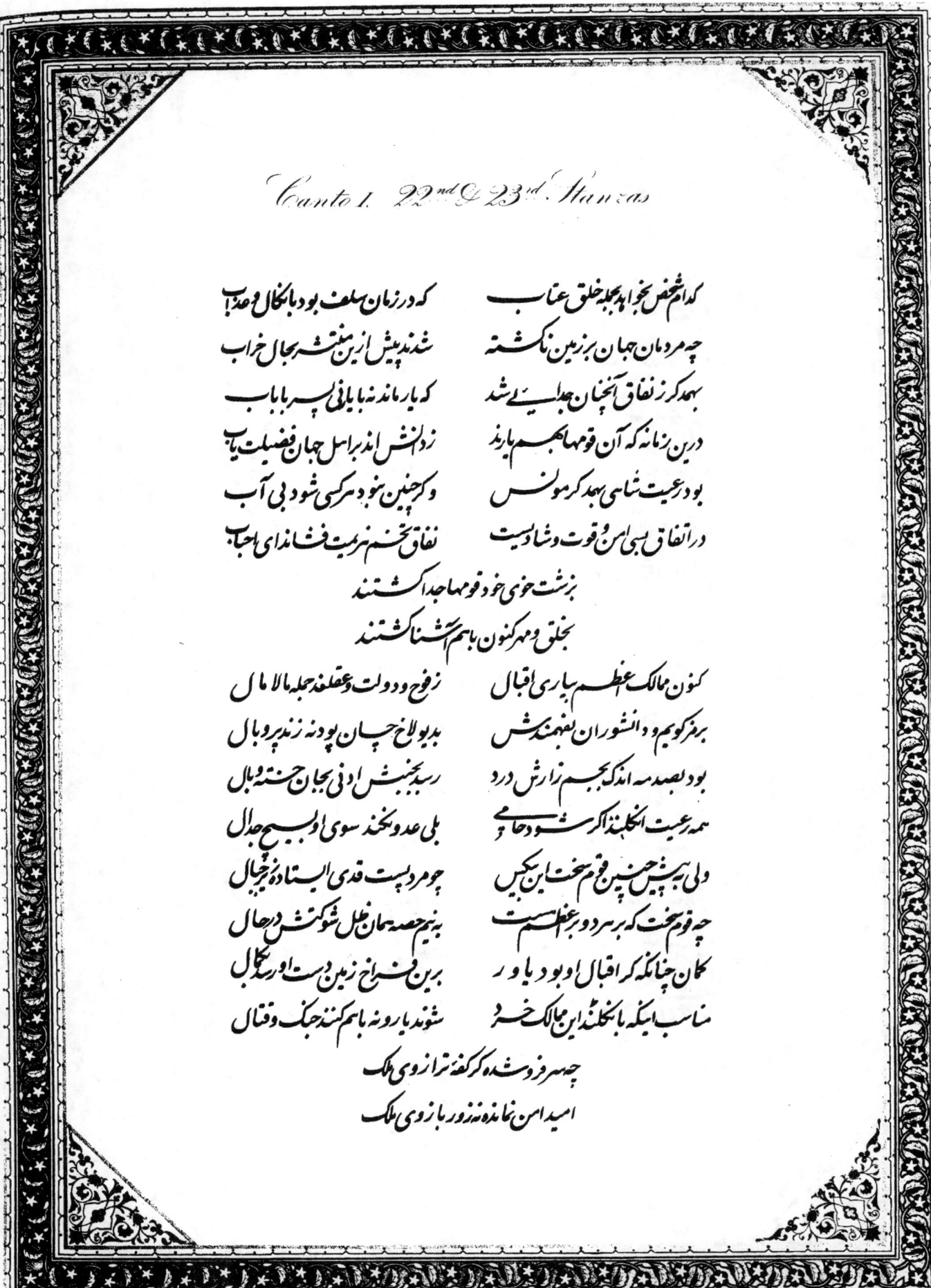

Canto 1. 24th & 25th Stanzas

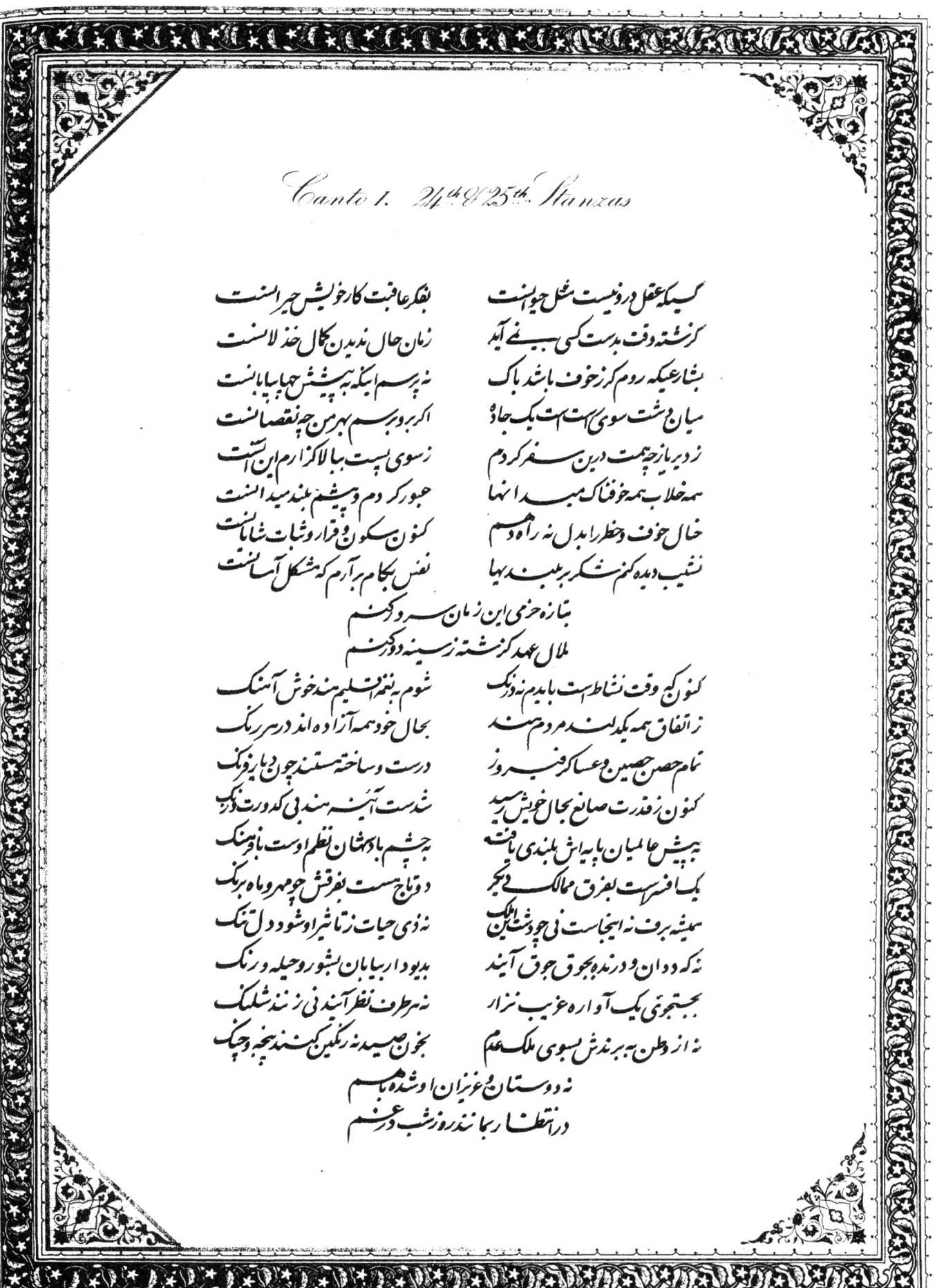

Canto 1. 26th & 27th Stanzas

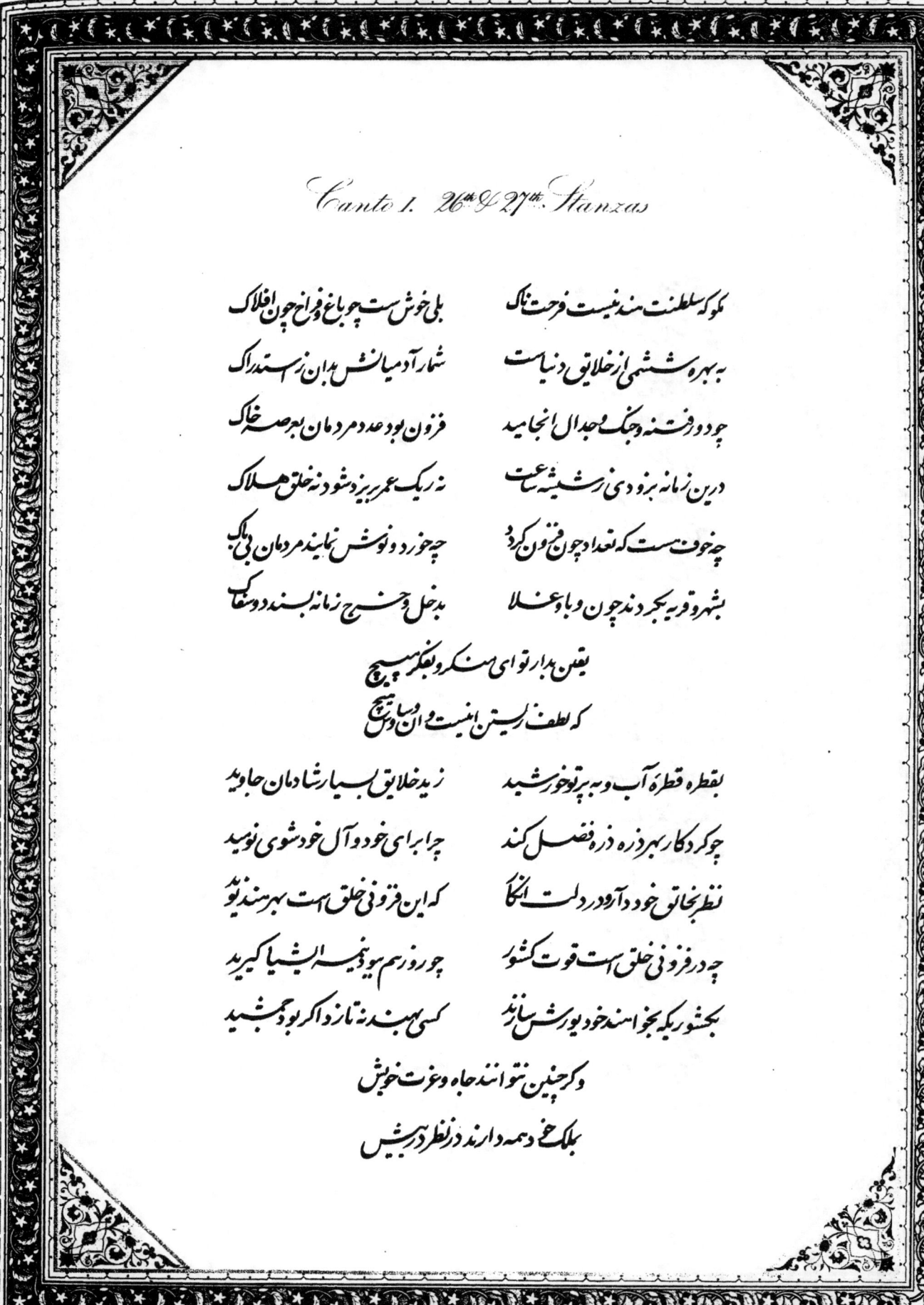

Canto 1. 28th & 29th Stanzas

چه زاد کہ موسیٰ خام درخیال آرد / چنین رعیت و کشور چو خسروی دارد

سحاب حق و برکت بہ ہندی بارد / سپاس حق کہ زفیض خزانہ معمور

نخو بیش کہ زمین دگر بسنکارد / بعرصہ کہ درو آب کلک گشتہ روان

ہزار دشت فرح بخش اگرچہ پیشباں / کسی نظیر نیاید بود بے کشمیر

ثنائی اوچو من پوچ گونہ نگارد / میان اوست چہ شہر کہ عقل حیرت است

ویا کہ شہر و نسْ را چو اوے بپردارد / طلسم ست آب غدیر او بہ جسم

قریب اوست یکی خرمی فن اکلزار

بوصف ست بہشت و بنام شالامار

بزِّ زمرد خوش رنگ ثبت کردیدہ / بر آن مین نہر کام سبزہ روئیدہ

بزیر سایہٴ عجیب سبزہ بالیدہ / لب غدیر زِ شیب اندر افراحنا

کہ بام و خانہ بالا و زیر سازیدہ / چنان کہ دور نما ید بدیدہ نخلستان

کسی چو دید ورا باغ عدن را دیدہ / نسیم باغ درنجا عجیب گلزار یست

لمک کہ لشکر دیوان لباس پوشیدہ / سفید برف نہ برقلہائی کوہ فتاد

کہ سینہ فلک معبرق سائیدہ / چہ سر بلند شدہ قلہائی مرتفعش

شگفت ایں کہ ہمہ آب سیم کردیدہ / زانعکاس ہمان قلہائی پر از برف

زعکس حسن وجمال بتانِ آئینہ رو

ہزار مہر درخشاں عجب جلوہ بود درو

Canto 1. 30th & 31st Stanzas

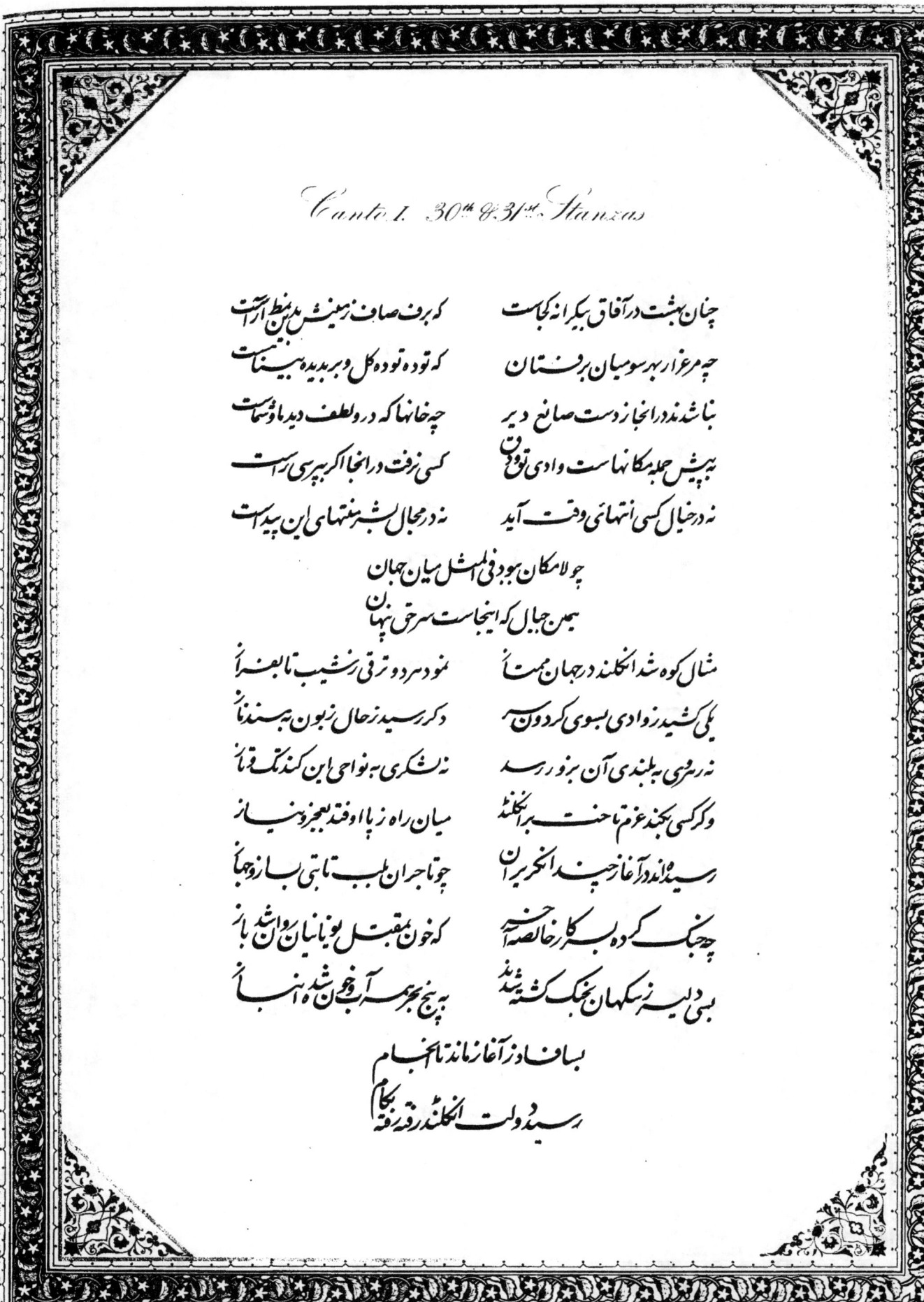

Canto 1. 32nd & 33rd Stanzas

چو سر کشیده بغاوت نه ارض تا بفلک   ز خون بجاری روان شد فزون از ان بشلک

چنان بانه زد مدر زمانه آتش مرک   که سوختند بسی اندر ان ز کودک

و فا شعار کسانیکه جسم و دل بودند   دریغ خورده بخفتند بر زن و طفلک

کز ظلم رفته بر انیان نژ ظالمان نسیم   کم که جمله فراموش کرده حق نمک

چه بیدریغ بهر قصد در زد ند آتش   چه بام و خانه حکام سوخت یکبک

چه اتفاق موذ مذبح جمله کبریشان   که نام و عزت بر زن شود زد نیا یکک

چو قهر کرده خدائی عت بر زود از زود   اسیر و خوار کشتند آنمه غرچک

نشان شکرانکلند زبهت بالا شد

به پیش از انکه تو کوئی فتاده از پا شد

مدت آمده دهلی آشکار شد   بهند این خبر فتح در شمار شد

کمان و هم مبدلهای ساکنانش ما   بهر دو چشم کسی خواب اکر ا شد

کسی نبود که بر پا نجست اندر خواب   فراغ را بدل و خاطری قرار شد

چه خوابهائی پریشان بنو در شب تا   سحر چو کشت کئی ظلمراز سرا شد

مدام برچم آن آفتاب جاه علم   ز با دام نجنبید و اعتبار شد

صلاح دید درین دم شهی کبی رایش   به نعمت و نقلات اندر ایح کار شد

که زیب تاج و لقب داد بر تقربت خویش   چه فری که بیک شاه زنهار شد

بهند مژده به نجبت که تاج قیصر یش   عزیز و ارجمندان که زنگ و عار شد

چه بوده ئی سرد و کوشش و تدبیر   چه انا بر یشان شور کار زار شد

کنون بهند بمه جنگ و فتنه آنجر کشت

که جمله مقصد الکلمند مست خلطه کشت

Canto 1. 34th & 35th Stanzas

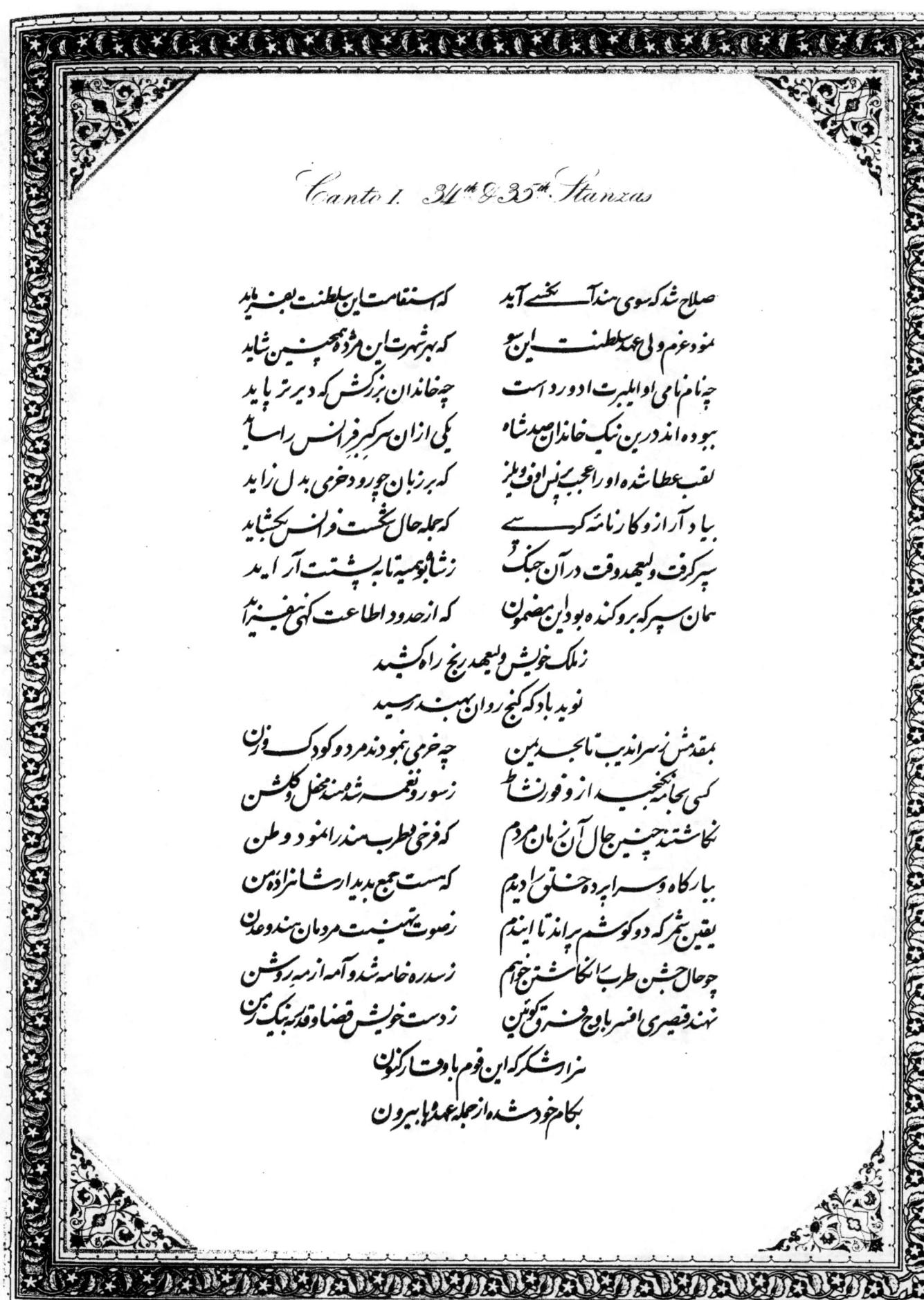

Canto II. 1st & 2nd Stanzas

و سلطنت نشمرد و کمت میان جهان   کسیکه کرد سفر در تمام هندستان
بعظمت به سی کمتری من فریدون   همه فرنگ و همه ملک او متعال تو
ضرورست برایت همین لقب شاهان   اگر حکومت والاست معنی این اسم
تمام سلطنت تو ماش بعین مقران   اگر به پهلوان ملک هند بنشینند
فروغ مهر دعا دهی شان نهان و عیان   به ارجمندی بخت تربیت کمترست
سه گونه زانهمه افزون کنی بیش چندان   توئی بعظمت و معموری و پهنائی

کرفتم افسر ایشان به پیش بهات
ولی مقابل و هم سم بی بهات کجا

که گیرد در خور خود مرتبه خلاف حسود   چحثم خوب برای تو بکلفت نمود
بدین وسطوت و اقبال و عز و جاه نو   چه رتبه بست که این قصرت باد
شوند از سرنوشت باجلال و صعود   عروج و عظمت و جاه شهان تیمور
تفاوتیکه بیابد بیان نمی نمود   ولی بعظمت که این و آنهمه شاهان
اگر سواحل آبست و گرچه خشک حدود   که جمله قبضه هندست و زیر فرمانش
شوند آمدن آن روز که جوشش سرود   زهی سواحل بحر یکه جمله یکجا
جدا حد انتوان کرد سمجو تا زرد   که بر رشته پیوند سنگ زرین
بهر زبان و به هر دم زیاد خواهد بود   ضرور شامل و خواهر سود ایشان

خیال خوف و کان کرد از میان نیل
بهمد گر نماین اتحاد و بدل

Canto II. 3rd & 4th Stanzas

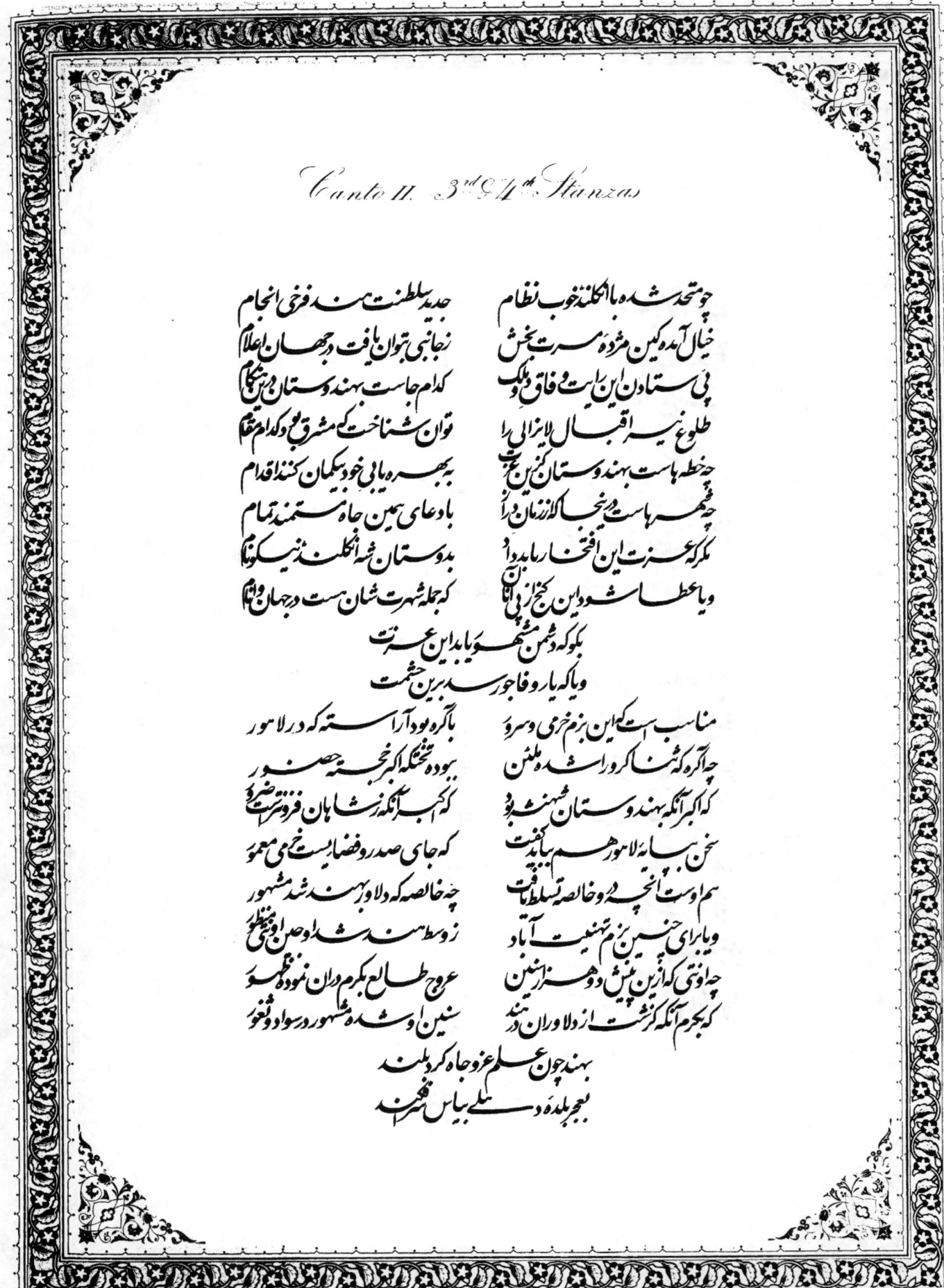

Canto II. 5th & 6th Stanzas

بلبل که در خور این جشن آمده متهرا
کز ازدبوم که کرشن حسین شد و اینجا

کرشن کو که ز خویش خمار باده حسن
مدام با سی و معشوقه کار بود او را

گرفته دست بتان جهان فریبنده
بسبزه زار بر قصه می آن بر عنا

بچشم سرکه شدی جلوه گر بقدرت او
همی نمود که او راست عاشق یکتا

نوای دلکش و بهتر از پیام وصال
که می ربود دل از شاهدان سیما

عجب که تیره نگارش بسینه عشاق
سرور و شوق همی کرد هر زمان پیدا

اگر بنا ز نمودی زد لبری انفعال
مسلم است که او راز جان شدی افشا

شد آن مقام که بازی گه کرشن حسین
با عقاد سنود آمده عزیز ترین

روان بدامن صحرا ست و به آنجا
سبزه هست عجب فرش مخملی بزین

بیاد او دل جانها بی سی خوانان خو
با وفسانه او کامشان شده شیرین

نه پاک است دگر جا چو به نزد منود
نه راست است چنان یک فسانه دیرین

بعهد دولت عیش کرشن خوش شد اقبال
کرشنه نیست کمایش سترگ زمین

سمان نشاط که شد منقلب بصورت خوش
کنون بسینه حکام کشتی رزین

بروح آدمیان ظل عقل طلی کشت
برفت پاک ز دلها کان و بیم کین

همین خوش است که آنجا بود چنین صفا
که یچ بلده نباشد چو او سرو قا

Canto II. 7th & 8th Stanzas

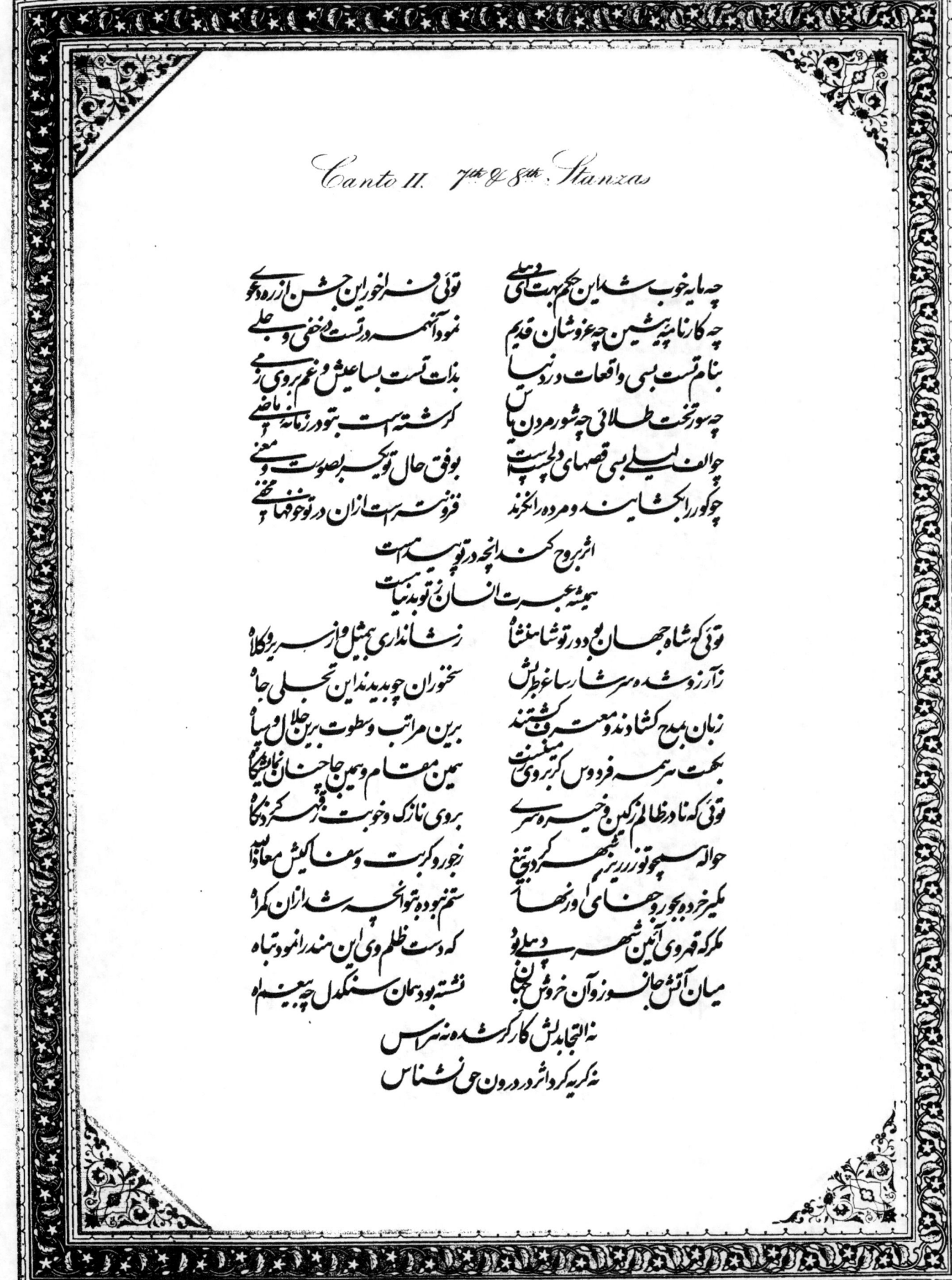

Canto II. 9th & 10th Stanzas

شد ست حادثۀ آنسری جی هیبت ناک   که خوف و قتل سر افراخته بعمۀ خاک
سمان بغاوت ملعون جی غول صحرائی   رسیدہ برسہ مردم بصوت ناپاک
قتیل خنجر کینہ وران ش اندریغ   بسی زنیکنهان آمدہ بعرض هلاک
نمود باسد ازین جان کسل و قیاعِ جنگ   کہ عقل گفت خود ازیم و شستش حاشا
بیاد او چو رسد حافظہ شدہ حیران   هزار بار رود پای او بہ نہرۂ مغاک
تصورش اگر آید بخاطرِ شخصے   پر از چهرۂ او رنگ کر بودی پاک
مورخی کہ نگارد زکر او حسرتے   زرس باز رود پای خامہ دل چاک
همین بست کزین خوفناک فسانہ   بہ نیزۂ کامی افتاد نغم بخزرم چالاک

بظلم خامشی و صبر باید ت کا
کہ ظالمی برسد خود بخیفہ کر دا

نبود باد وران روزتن چون صخر   بخاطری بشری هم نبود خطورشر
نشان و پرچم انگلن زیان بہ بارۂ شہر   ستادہ بود بہ بالای راست مثل شجرہ
کہی زنیزۂ چو ماربزرگ پیچیدہ   کہی فسردہ چواندر خسان کل احمر
کہی چو مردہ لیسی جنگ دیدہ   شدہ زحرب شبانروز کامل مضطر
ز وقت سرہ شدن تی پ صبح تا ہشم   بدر ز نعرہ و افغان نبود ہیچ اثر
بروج و مسجد و دیوانِ خاص و خندق و   ز تابش خوری بود کرم مثل شہ
تمام امن و ست عافیت بہر جاود   چو دشت و کوہ و سیاباں چی شہر ولاگز
بداشتند ہمہ اتفاق در دلہا
کہی نبود خیالِ نفاق در دلہا

Canto II. 11th & 12th Stanzas

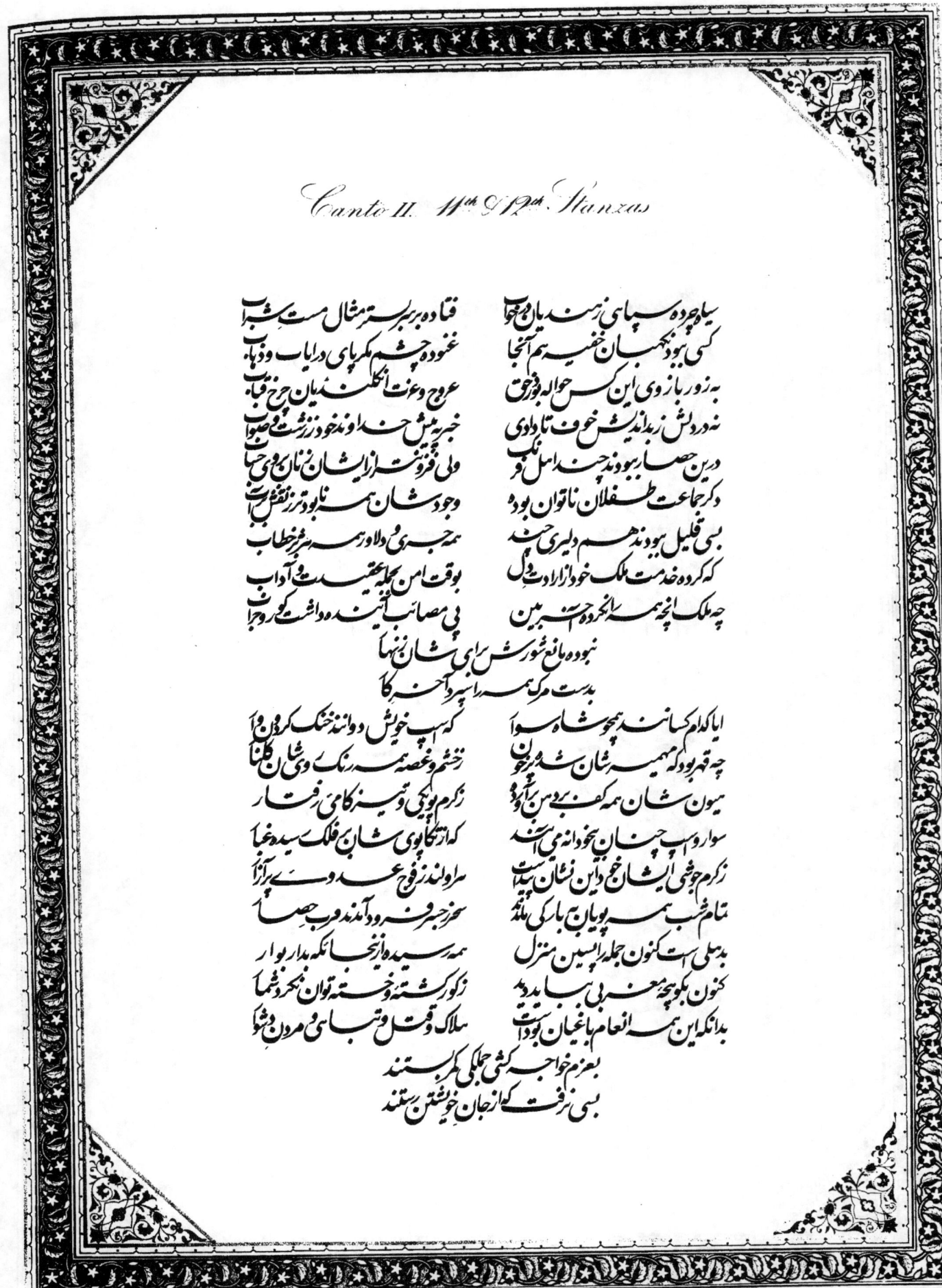

Canto II. 13th & 14th Stanzas

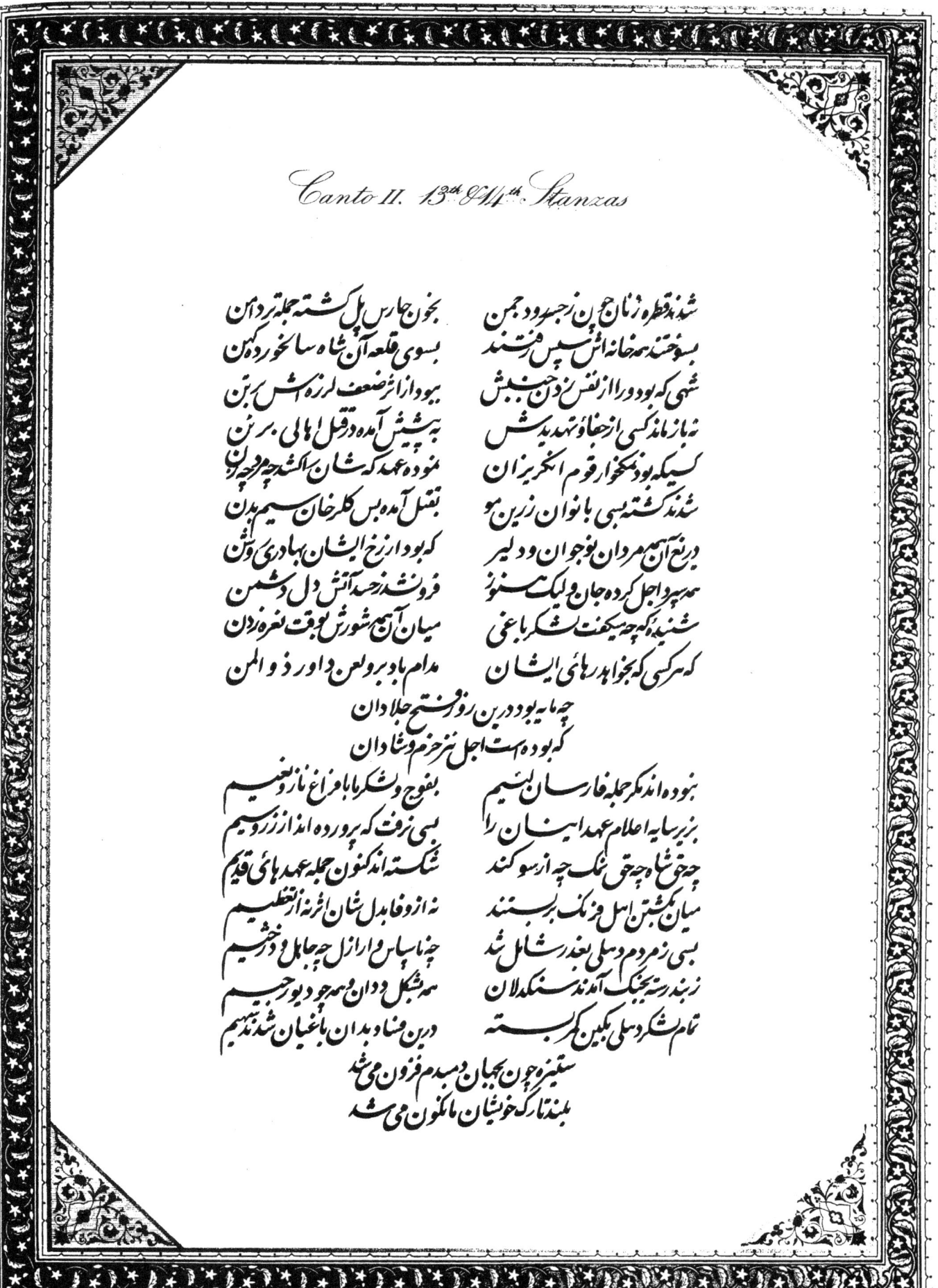

Canto II. 15th & 16th Stanzas

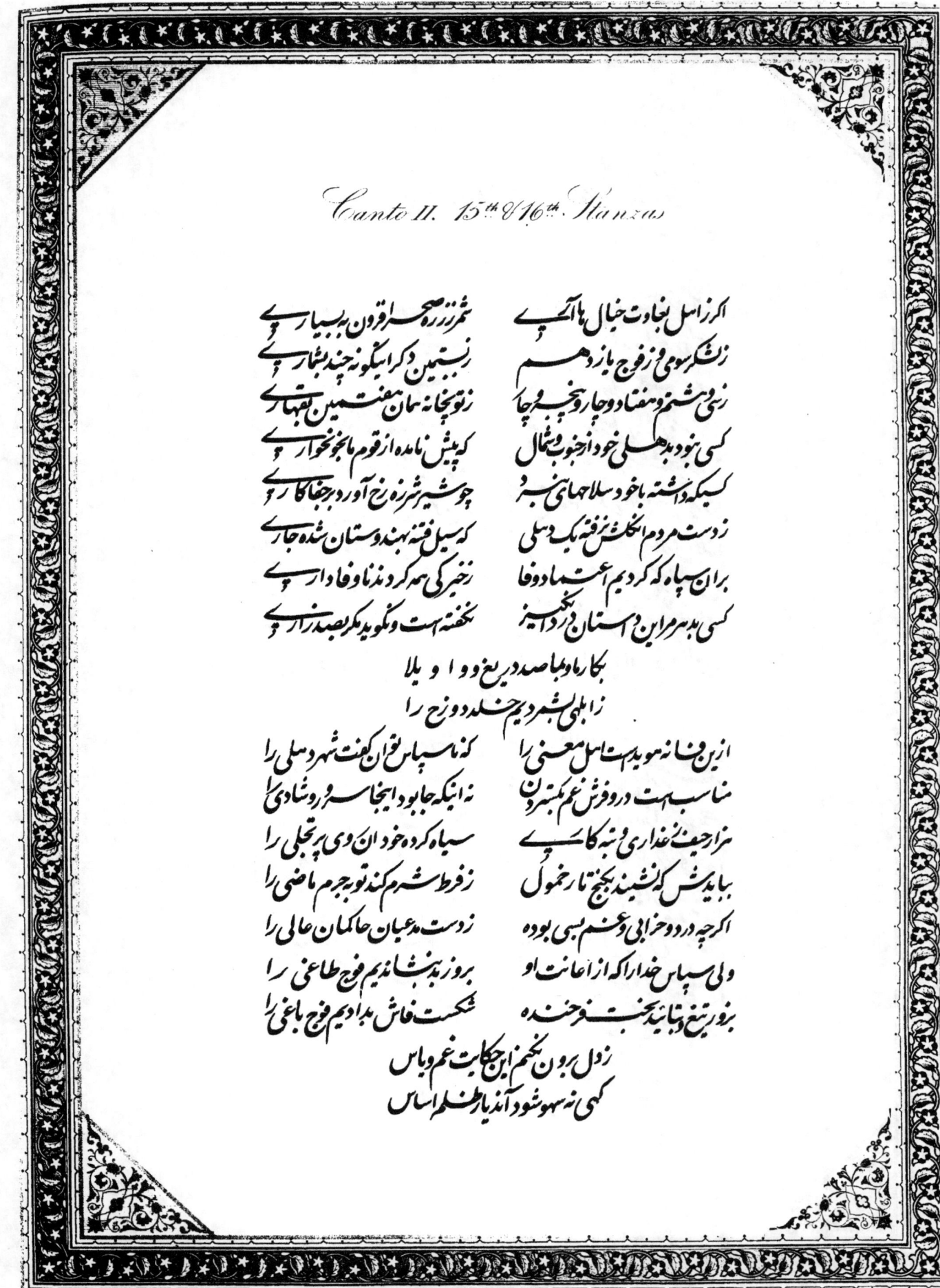

Canto II. 17th & 18th Stanzas

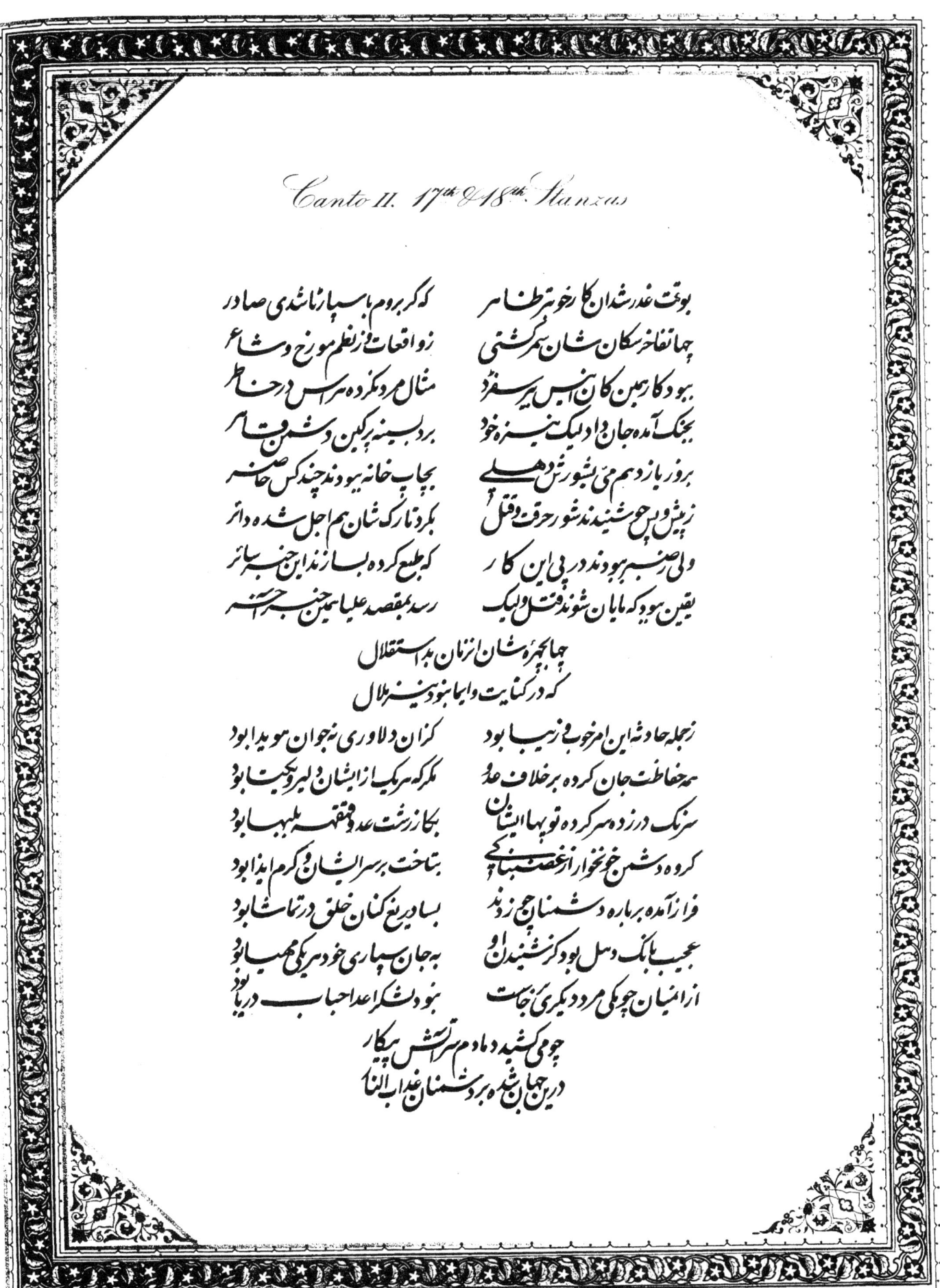

Canto II. 19th & 20th Stanzas

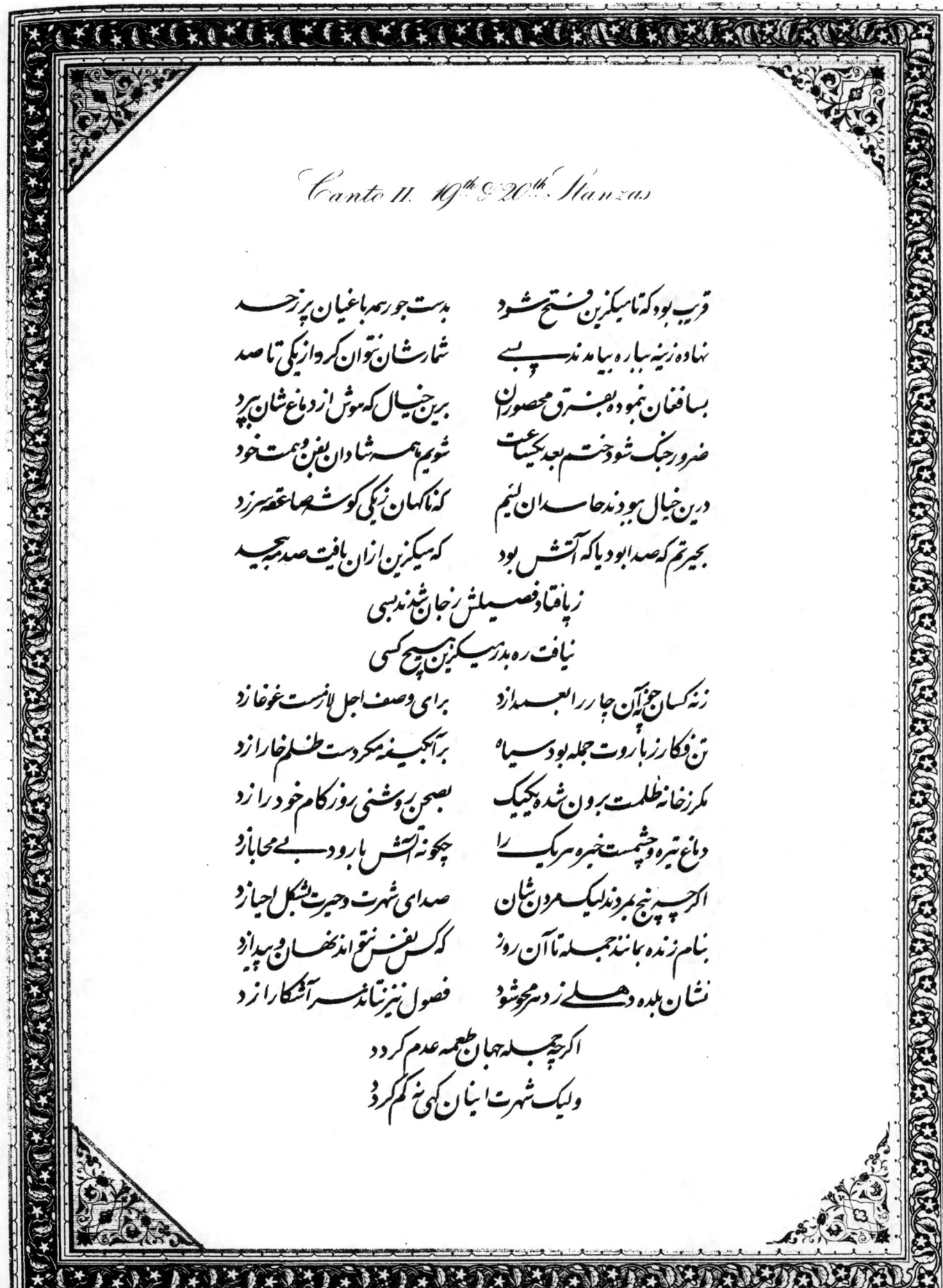

Canto II. 21st & 22nd Stanzas

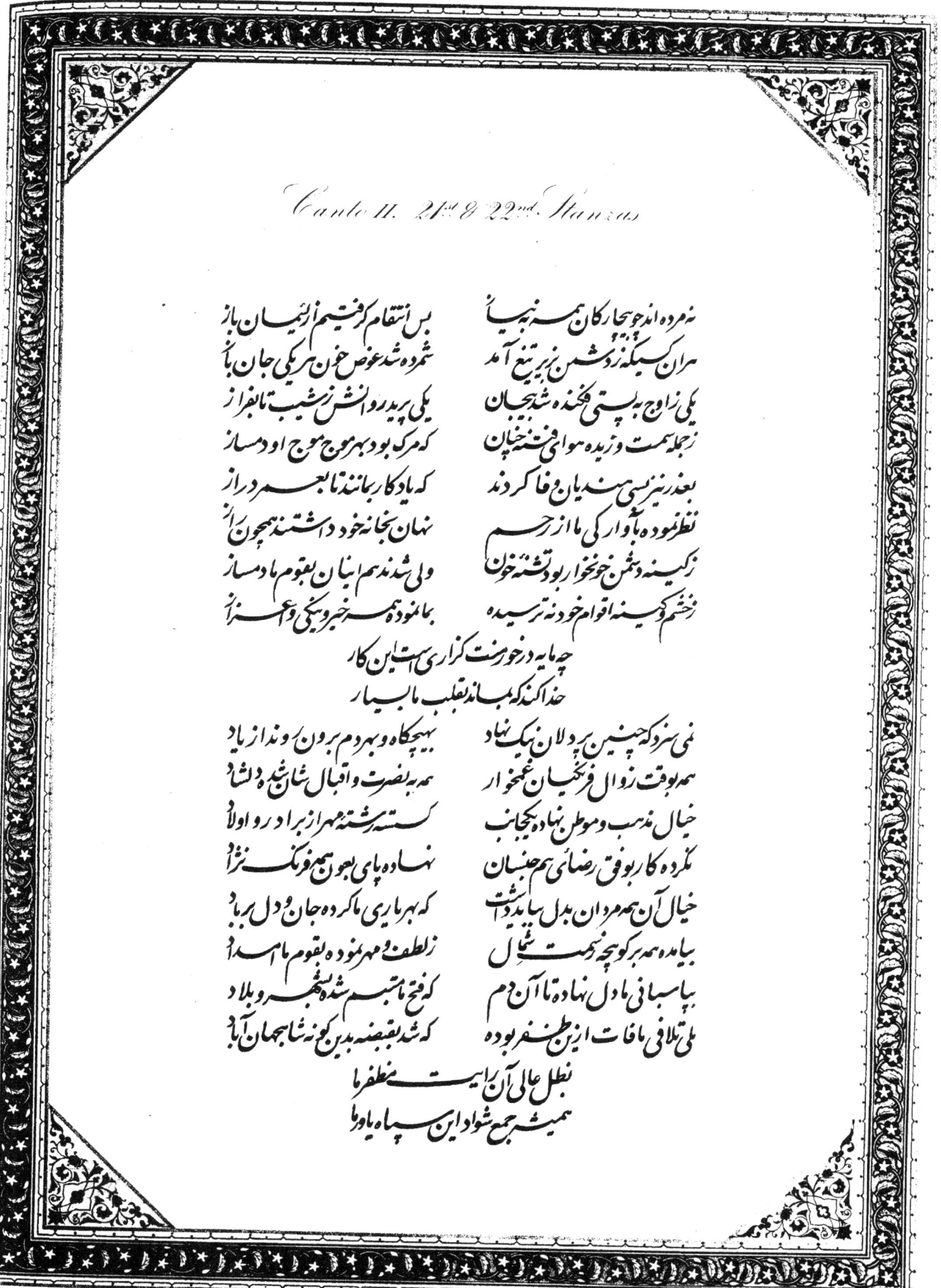

Canto II. 23rd & 24th Stanzas

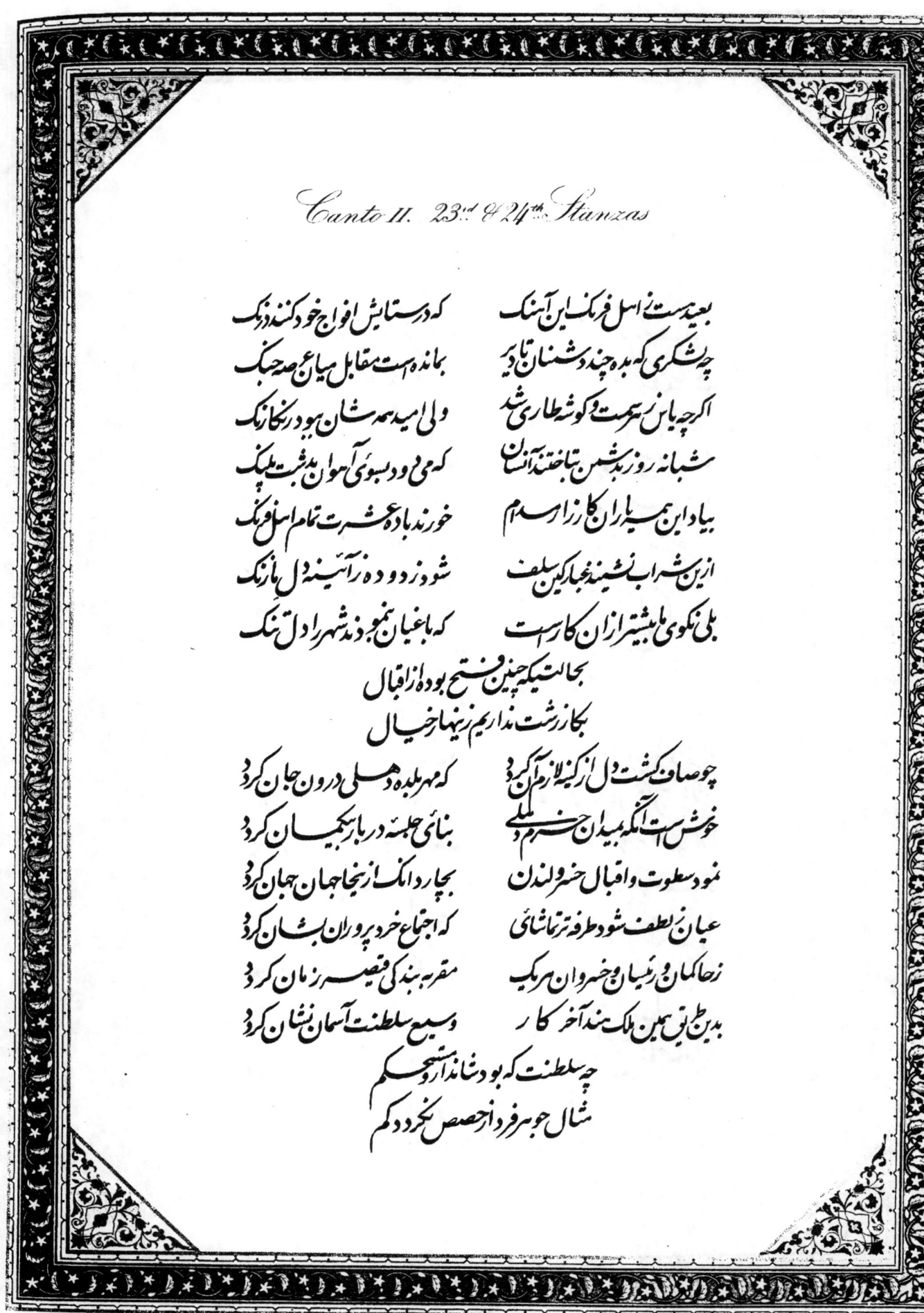

Canto II. 25th & 26th Stanzas

زهی مقام سرت فراز میانش   که جمله وسعت و دحت بخشد جهانش
نموده‌ایم ازو عبرت فنا حاصل   بوقت دیدن آن کوشهای ویرانش
چنانکه یک بجهر المحل نقل جابحند   مدام است تغیر بکهنه بنشانش
بگیر این سبق از آن معابد کهنه   که نیافت توان نام صاحب خانش
نخو جانب آن قلعه‌های دیرینه   که شد کنامه دد و بوم و حوش و اوانش
همه ساجد کهنه که منهدم کشتند   دریغ است که یک یک قالب دانشش
چه قهر بود که ناشی یک دعا نشد   دم تپاسی آن خانهای و سامانش

چه قدرت است معابد بنا مکلده کرد
در و بجای سمن غنچهای دشت دید

این جا به نظر ان پیوست شرق و شمال   چه قصه است که کوی حصار با اجلال
بزیر قلعه روان کشته است و روشن بیال   پاسبانی و مست و روشن بیال
زدگشانی و بروز بهار او پیداست   که تخت شاهی جهان و اندران جلال
مرقع ایست بهارش خیال شاعرا   چه شاعر یکه بود نغز کوی ملک خیال
بلند است در بیوند و صد فیت   فصیل مخندق او محکم و فراخ نها
خهی دور فصیلش که بتوان گفتن   دو لشکر است مهیا برای جنگ و جدال
همه بروج بلند و وسیع دمدمه هاش   که نیکی بفلک سر کشیده و مج جبال

میان این دو فصیل است مدما آبا
سین دو سه است که بود در شاه جهان آبا

Canto II. 27th & 28th Stanzas

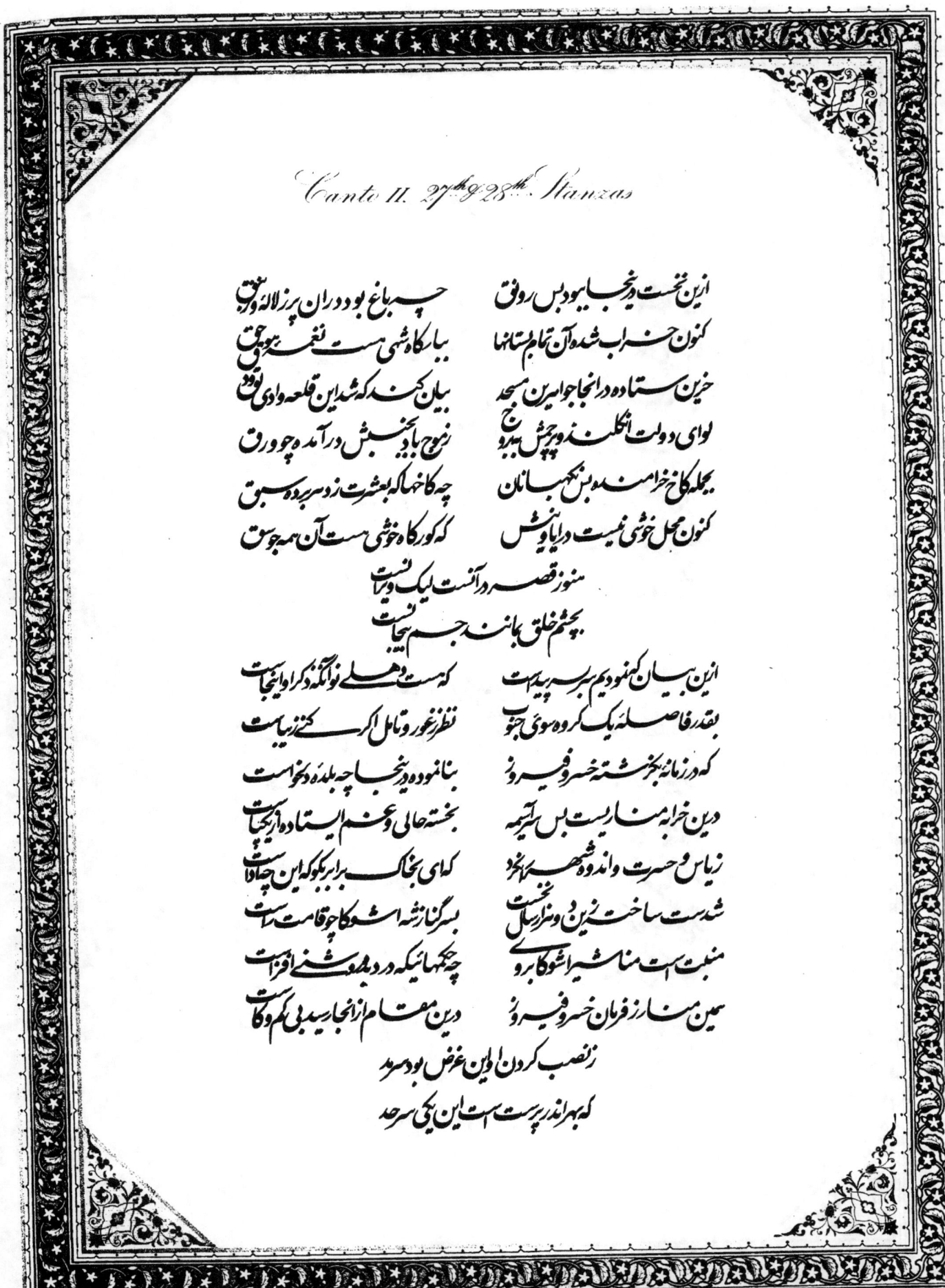

Canto II. 29th & 30th Stanzas

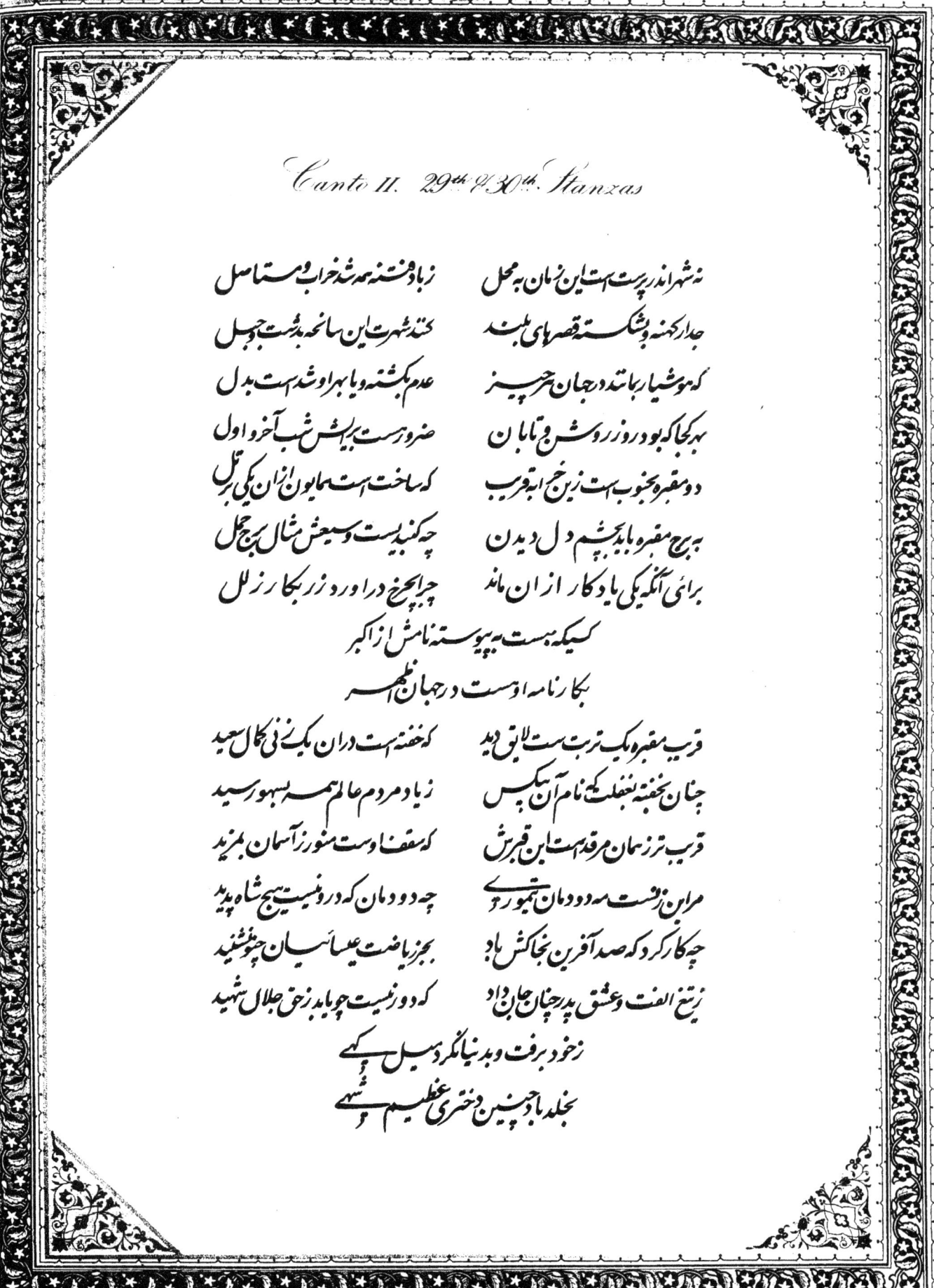

Canto II. 31st & 32nd Stanzas

بسوی قبروی از غور یک نگاه بس است که صرف نام وی اینجا زجمله جاه بس است
نبشته است چه بر تربت جهان آرا که بهر عبرت دلهای پر گناه بس است
کسی که رحم بیک ذره در دلش نبشد بیحیی وسگ از دربک واو بس است
نه سقف است زر زور خام بر قبه ش همین کتابه درین جا ور اپناه بس است
بنبیر سبزه نپوشد کسی مزار مرا که قبر پوش غریبان همین کیاه بس است

چو دوست داد مر این زن بخانوا ده بهشت
بحق شیخ بدست آمدش قصور بهشت

بر وسمت جنوبی این عبد تربت ببین چه یفت حصار ندا بامه وسعت
بوصف خوبی درگاه قطب این ژیا فتاده ام زره ولشکر در کوه حیرت
ستاده هست در اینجا مناره ی صفت گرشته فوقی از آسمان زبین رفعت
نه بیجواست مناری به صرو دیگر جا که مشبه بجهان است در نامه صفت
اگر بقبله تعلق نظر کنی دل که تاچه بود و چه شد حالتش درین مدت
دکر بقبره اش چشم دل کشاده شود زذر و حیف در آید بدل نبی رفت
درست نسبت که اینجا بنا نهاده شود برای حسن نو و ستوار و خوب بیت

خراب و خسته عمارات و بوم و یرانه
نه لایق است به ترتیب بزم شاهانه

Canto II. 33rd & 34th Stanzas

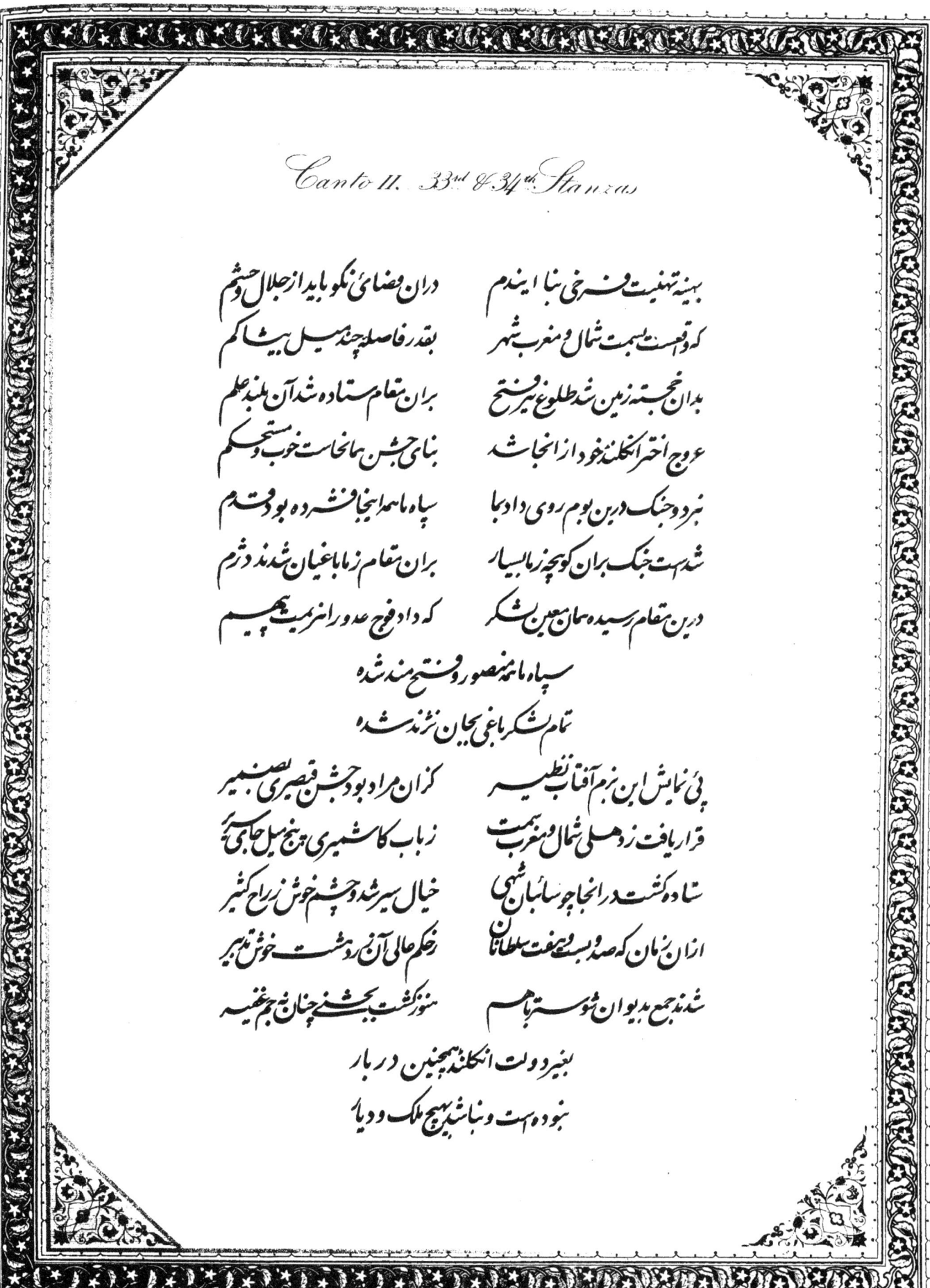

Canto II. 35th & 36th Stanzas

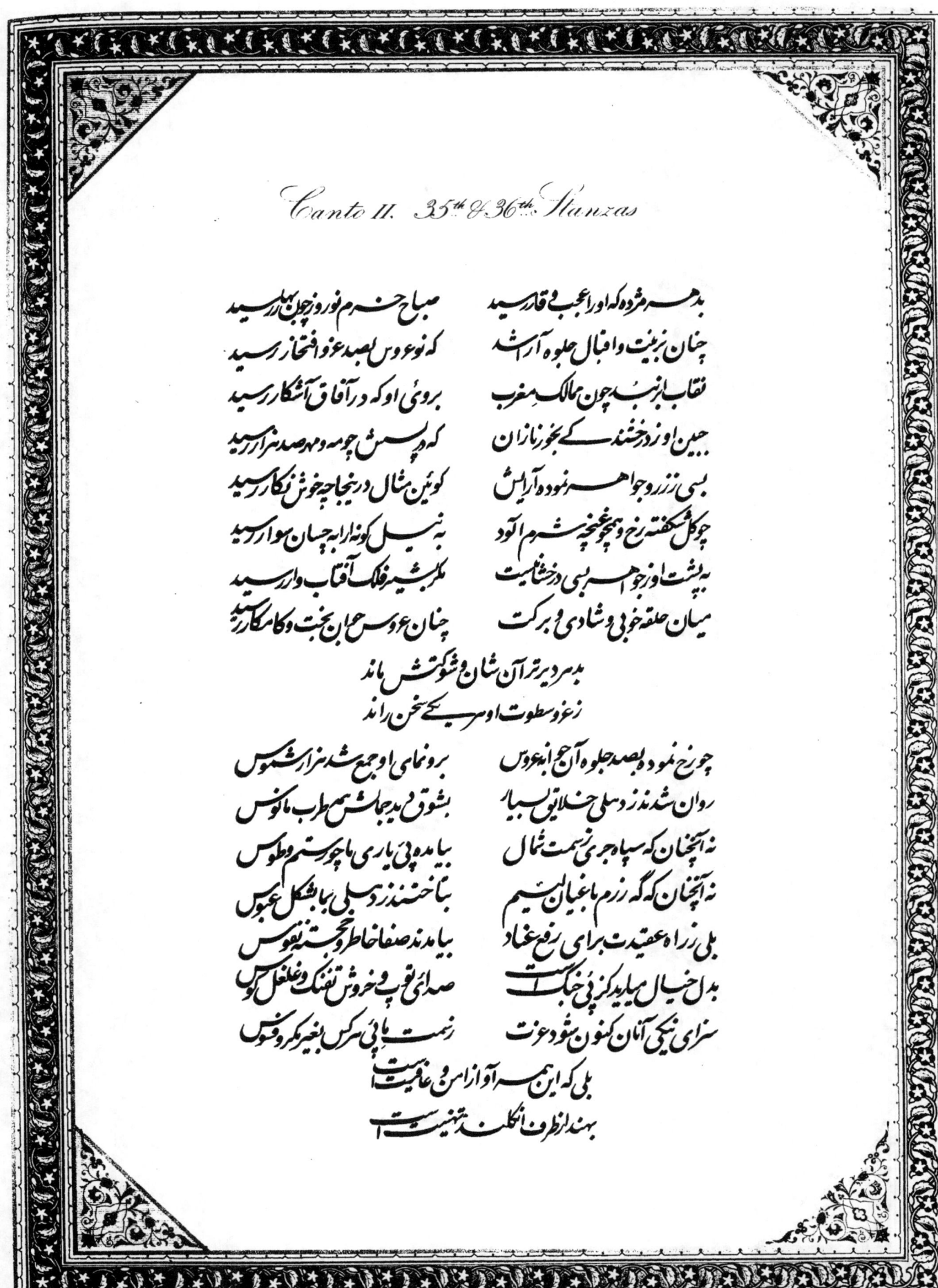

Canto II. 37th & 38th Stanzas

روان شدند چو مردم به بزم باندبنائے زدیدشان سنجیر ببا ند بنائے

بجوق جوق لباس کران به تن کردہ بیامدند تماشائیان بزیبائے

بیامدند رئیسان با چشم بسیار ہمه سوار بر اسپان بجمله رعنائے

روان شدند رئیسان کو سرین طبوس سہ بہ پیل نشسته بجلوه آرائے

خرام داشت بآہستہ ترجان بر پیل کہ شد نه مانع رہرو کوہ بالائے

اگر شتاب نمودندی آنهمه پیلان

چه پایمال شدندی براه پیر و جوان

روان شدند زکیک سمت پرده دارائے کہ جلگی بہاری بدند با شانے

شدند پردہ درخ خلق جمله در پردہ زہر نگاه و زہر غمزہ و زہر آئنے

کمی بنازبسی جلوه حسن خود کردند زہی سلیقہ نگاہی نگاهبازانے

روان بود بخرو نه نیبه بنائے کہ نه بہی بخشش زکا و نادانے

سیاه فامہ بود او چو رخ غنچہ کہ مدام ہمی فروخت بسود و زیان یک کانے

روان بدند بر ہ اشتران قطار قطار باآن خرام که طاؤس درگلستانے

فرخشتند ازان اشتران عنق سرگاه

کہ عزر کردہ درا نبوه با زنند براه

Canto II. 39th & 40th Stanzas

رسید راه بیابان و انعام آمد   که سایبان ثنائی خاص و عالم
کسی ز مردم هندی محمود صحبت بود   اگرچه برفلک خور و راقیام آمد
بلی به بزم شگفتی فنا اکبر نخست   با بتسام ثنایش بجه کلام آمد
ولی نظر چو نمود نزد بارگاه شهی   بچشم و چهره شان از خوشی پیام آمد
تمام خنده و زنان پیش از انکه سریک را   فلک بدست رسید و جهان بکام

بسوئی دیگر آیا بدین نظر چو فگنند
ز ترتیب وی چه تعجب بدل در آنحمند

ازان بدند مه سایبان بشکل هلال   که بود از پی شان و زیب جلال و جمال
بدر میانه یکی خیمه وسیع بود   به عنز و دبدبه و فر و دولت و اقبال
سران رئیس که برپشت بارگاه نشست   به تختگاه رسیده نگاه او بکمال
منور تخت که خوب چون دل صنمی   ز نقش غیب تهی بود و پر ز جاه و جلال
ولیک جمله رئیسان دران هلائی نم   بیامدند و نشستند شاد و نیکو حال
بکمر دتارک سریک رئیس استاد   بسی عماید دانش پیشه و خیر سگال

بعز و شوکت سریک بود آن شایان
که خود طلب نماید نشان هندستان

Canto II. 41st & 42nd Stanzas

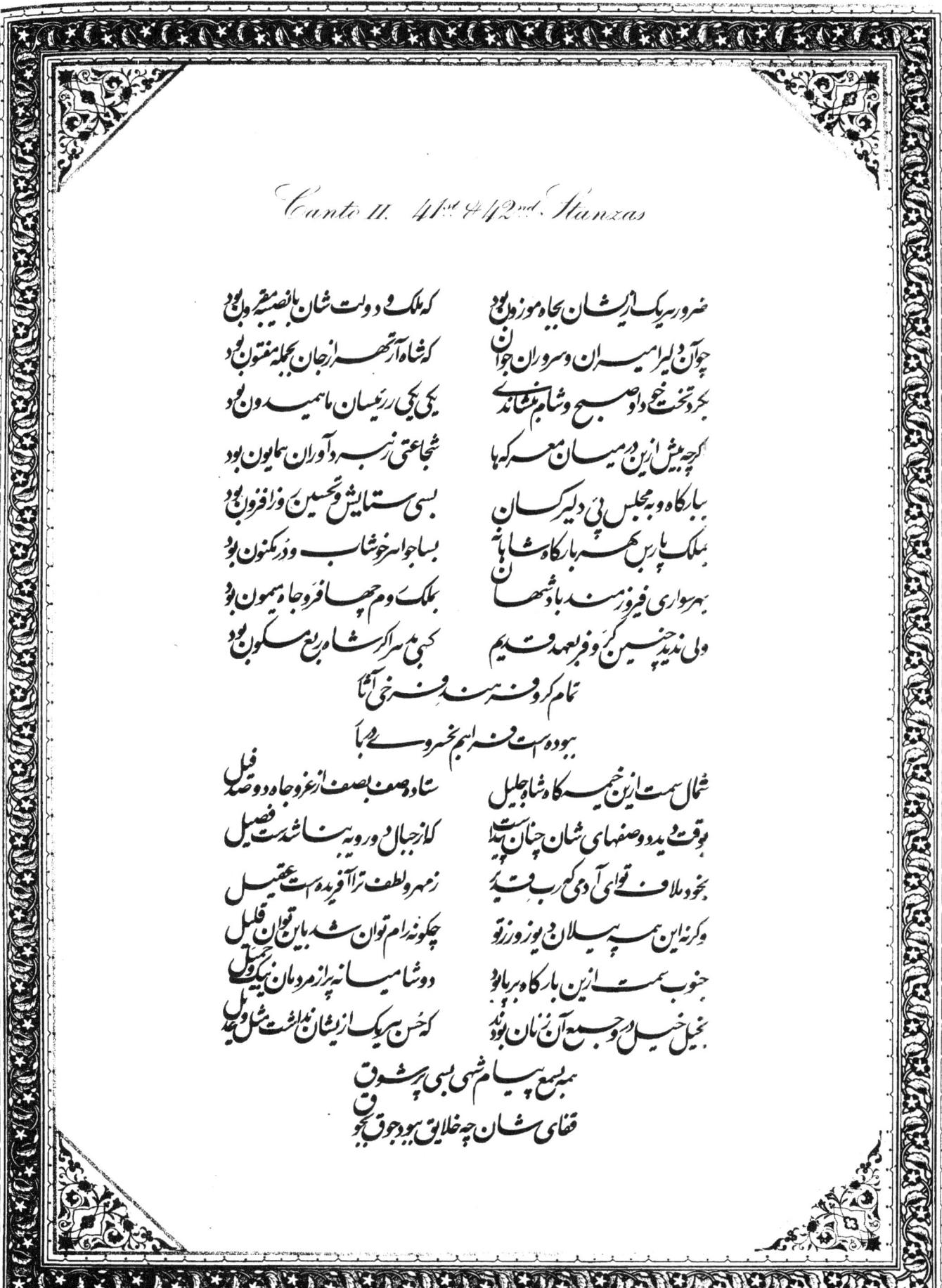

Canto II. 43rd & 44th Stanzas

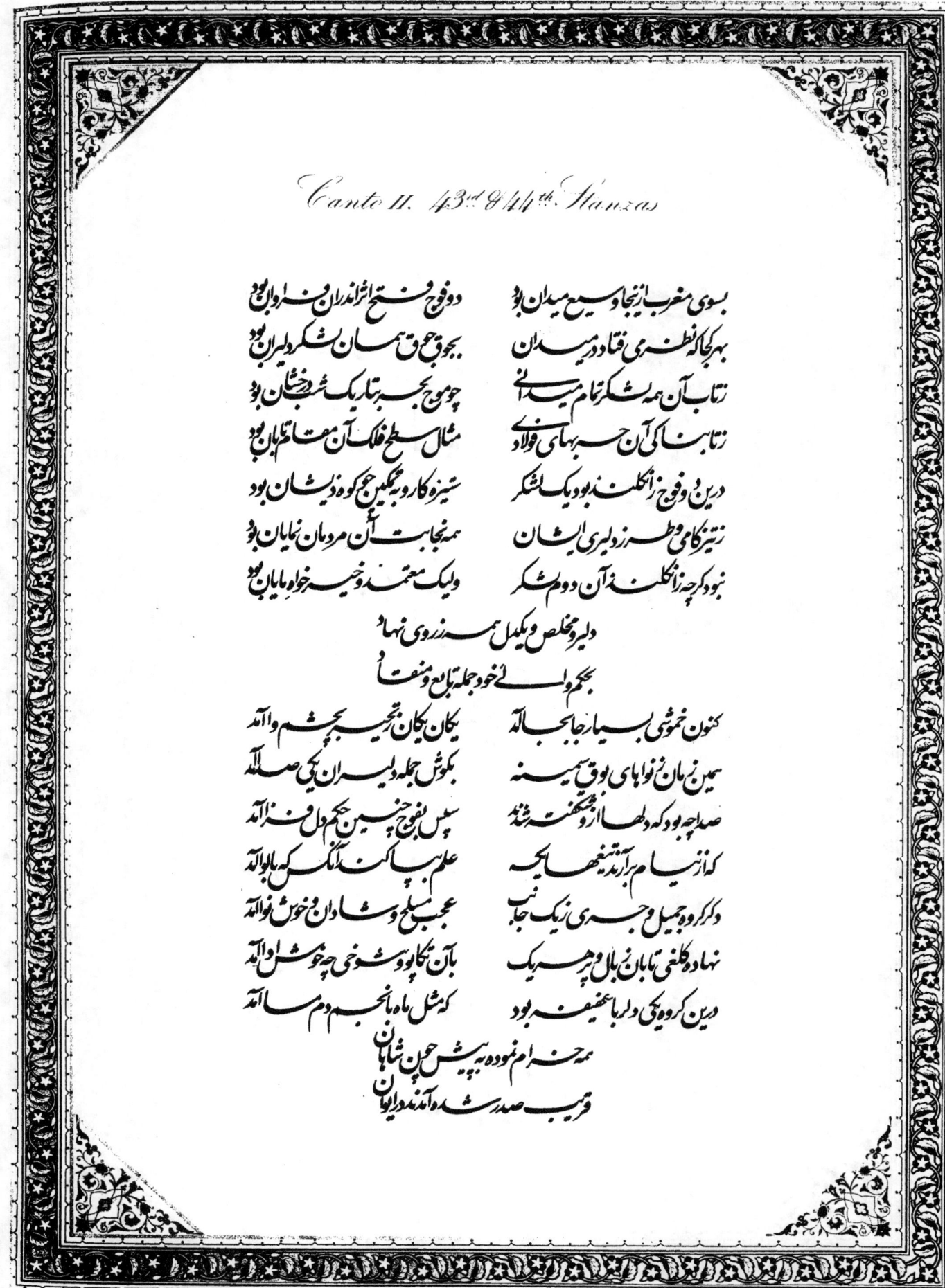

Canto II. 45th & 46th Stanzas

کدام بود درین ساعت مجسته اساس / بغیر حاصنری آن کوئین چرخ هماس
که او به تخت شهی جلوه گری باشد / بحکم گشاء وانشور بلند قیاس
چه شاعری که مر او خلق گشته ازلی آن / که میر مجلس شان بود و شکوت و یاس
چه حاکمی که هدایت کند به عالمیان / بان بلند خیالی بفیض عقل و حواس
هم اوست به حکم ذرم قلب حق نشاس / که حکم او بحکم این جاه و منزلت آری
ببر شان بوی د آنکه نجم و نور غلاب / که نور عقل کند دور از درون وساس
صبح و بخیر دو عالی شکوه و بناست / زید دهر بآسودگی و خوش انفاس
بغیر لازدلت کیست درین عیان و نهان / معین خلق و خلایق مدام صرف سپاس
شود خلق چنان حکمران زحکمت خویش
که ناکواز انباشد بدوست و بد اندیش

خرام داشت زن چون پری بهکلامش / سبز بچهره او کرکو این بود نامش
بحن همچوزن شاه و آنکه نیک انجامش / زیاده بود ازان عقل نیک انجماش
نصرف قامت او بچو سرو موزون شبه / خدا بجبت بقالب تمام اندامش
درست اینکه زجاد وی چشم او صرم / بسی شجاع و بسی پادشاه در و امش
چه آدمی که مجال سروش چندان نیست / که زان عنیف بر آرد بسجکه کامش
چو او حلیم و شریف و خلیق و چو حب جمال
کسی ندید و کز زن باین صفات کمال

Canto II. 47th & 48th Stanzas

باین مان کم خوشی در جهان نمایان شد   نظام انجمن قیصری بشایان شد

چو جلوه کرد به تخت آن کوہ زر والا   تعقیب آمد و قائم شوکت و شان شد

لوای جلوه یسان بجبای خود آنا   مثال پرتو خور آن مان درخشان شد

ازین نویدم دران زدم قلب مہ حاکم   مثال غنچه سخت و چو باد جنبان شد

ایا کدام ست به آنکه تعبیر نیش   نخست لازمه فکرت سخندان شد

کدام ست نشسته درین ہلالی جا   کہ پیش تخت شمی عنیش و لوا شد

کدام ست که از نظم مدہش الکنوں   چنان بہ نغمہ الغاب و شہ مفتوں

نخست نغمہ اقبال حضرمی پیو   سرود و مست بانگلند با دل خرسند

سپس بنا بر آنکہ در ہلالی سنا   نشستہ بود چو نور شہان بہ تخت بلند

ذخیرہ اش ہمہ خوبی و مہ پر سیلاو   بدست آمدست عجب خطہ طرب کند

وسیع تر زا طالیست کشور ش کہ دران   تمام خلق بہ بخشش بی ارادہ تمند

بجدہ ملکتش تا حکومت قصیہ   شود کشادہ بہ رو مثال جبل کمند

مجال نیست کہ دشمن بہ بوئی وہ بند   ویاور ابر ساندر ہیچ کونہ کزند

بجدہ ملک نظام انجمی سہ بخوا

کہ تی تخت کنند ملک قیصہ فریبا

Canto III. 1st Stanza

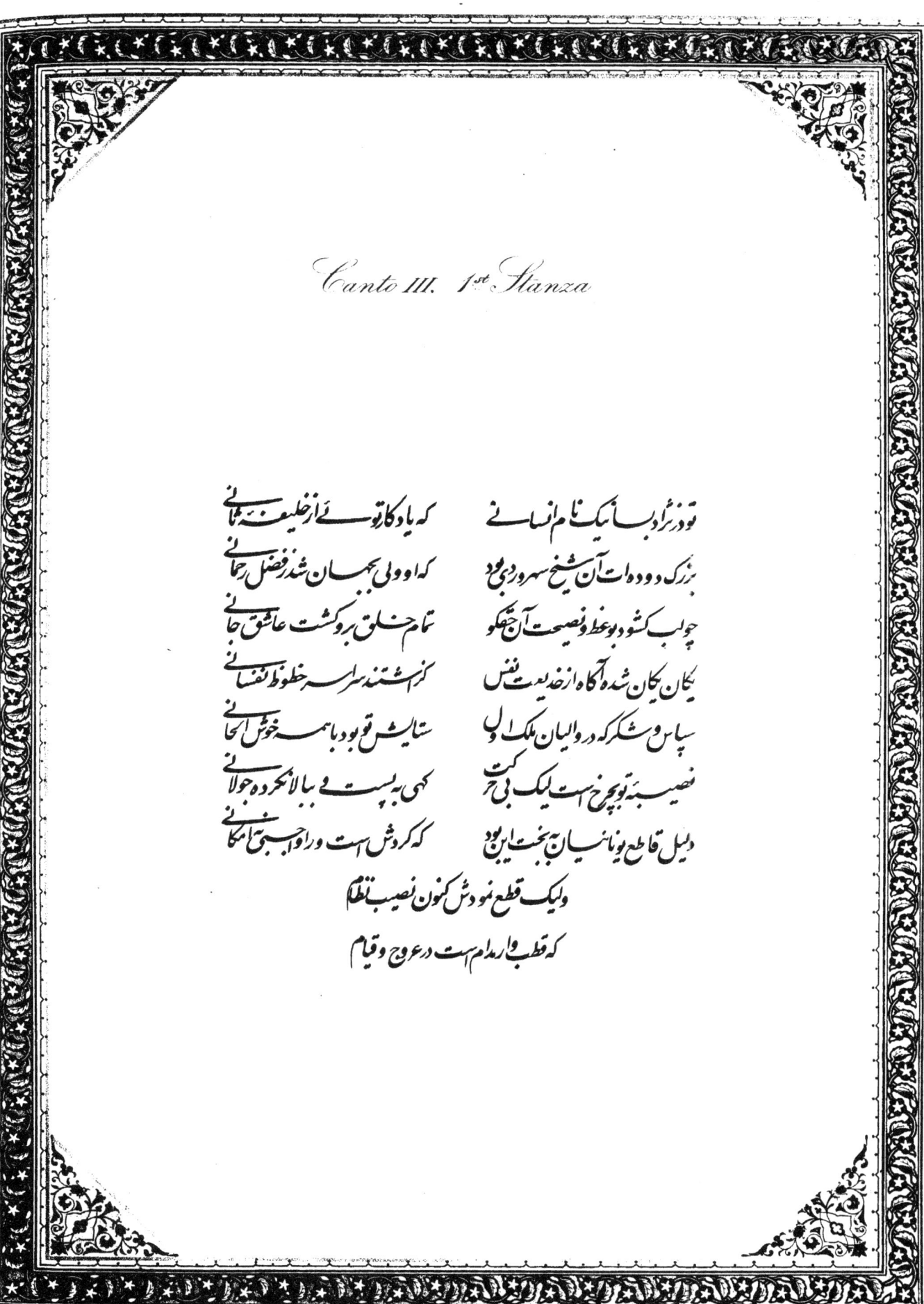

Canto III. 2nd & 3rd Stanzas

ولی و شاه که بسی اشرف نسب داری   و آن امیر که چون خسروان حسب داری

که زرنگار بر و آنهم لقب داری   کسی نه محمود نام نیک شان زعلم

که نام بزرگان بصد ادب داری   بدین نام بلندت چنان موقت بنا

که ملک و مال ز میراث جد و اب داری   دعای نیک بزرگان توست مقبول

توقع باب لعالم ازان سبب داری   چو آن بزرگ تو در راه حق ریاضت کند

مه نکوئی او بر علم مزین شد

همه شکوه در اولاد او مبرهن شد

چو تار و پود و کسته ز هم جدائی شد   بملک سند بد و پاره پادشائی شد

نظم و کنش آنهمه کیائی شد   بدست خسرو دهلی بماند نیک نیمه

رنا بخش نه کهی این کره کشائی شد   بجز است شاه مغل ملک قبضه گیر بنا

که در دیار دکن جمله نارسائی شد   بملک سند سراسر نماند عظمت او

بسر زمین دکن خوب و شنائی شد   دو پاره کرد چو نقت پر سند را آن وقت

قاده پاره والاس زافر شاهی

بهائی و بدکن داد شاه بجائی

Canto III. 4th & 5th Stanzas

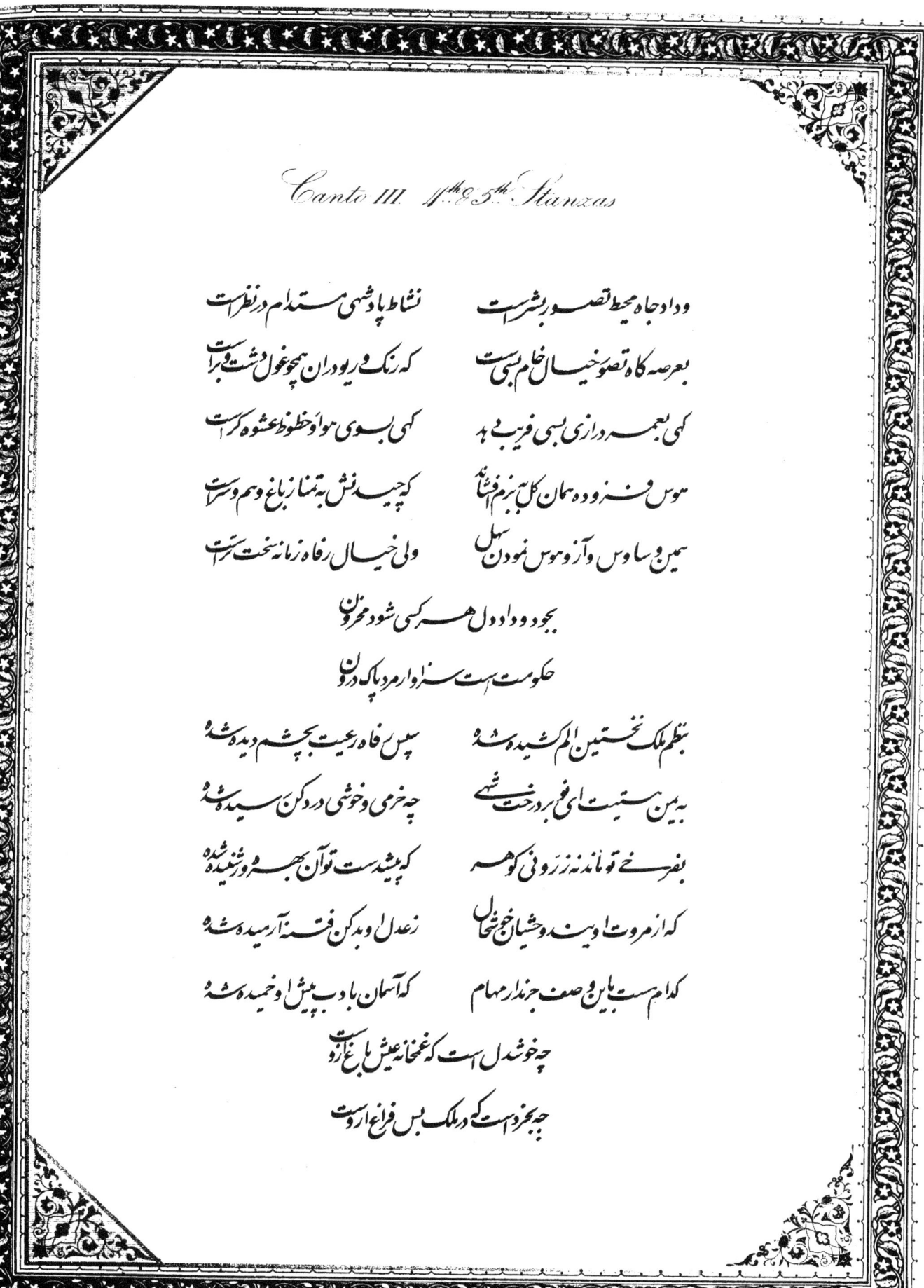

Canto III. 6th & 7th Stanzas

بیامده زمینـی یکی زآبـایش که نوبهـیر عرب آن بزرگ یکتـایش

بسی برآید و نهـان شود بدنیامهر زدل نه محو شود و لیکـ نام والایش

چه روشن است زنظمش زمین بیجاپور که مهـروار فروزان شده در وریش

چگونه محو شود نام او رسینه بخلق که واقعات مزین شد از ثنا هـایش

زال و همه دیوان نمـه بیجاپـور چنان شـدند که آن خطه یافت آرایش

بحق جمله بسی شاعران ثنا خوانند

بلوک کردن این ساز بس سخن رانند

گرشتم از سر وصف همه که یک بینم بمدح سنبـی یک شخص فـوکـی آیـنم

سمان کس است دین خطـه دکن نامـی بس است وصف چنان شخص بهترینم

علی الله دوام سر آید مدح سر سالار جمیع ملکـ دکن نغمـه خوش آئینم

بغارتار نشده ته چوپارسا داند کـمن زخـلق کریزم از آن کـمـی بینم

عبادتی کنم و روزهـا بسی دارم روم بجنگـلد زطوبی فواکـه چینـم

همین کس است بدنیا زسیر عالم ده که پرشکسته و داند که مثل شاهینم

یقین شمار که دنیا مقام معرفت است

به ترک کردن او نیز خوف عاقبت است

Canto III. 8th & 9th Stanzas

بطفلی تو شده ای شه دکن مشکل / که خود کنی بر عایا توجه کامل

غم و ترس دلها چگونه دور کنی / بکارهای خلایق چسان شوی مایل

بکار مالی و سلکے بباید ت شخصی / که بار خلق خدا را بسر بود حامل

سفینه های سران و کن بساحل من / چنا خدا برساند بهو شیاری لل

نظام لازم مختار است ملزوم / پس خطاتے بر نام او ست دل مایل

چه عزت بهتے و کن را بحال و استقلال

ازین وزیر و ازین پادشاه نیک خصال

بوده اند دهلی بسی شهان نامی / گزشته اند در دنیا همه بنا کامی

بخا نواده چغتائیان چنڈ روز بود / ولیک مانده آنهم بر شت انجامی

سمان کسانکه بدانش کار بن شنند / مرده اند بزود بے رنحس آنامی

ولیک سلطنت یا زنیک باطن ما / شد استوار ز آغاز تا بفنجر جامی

مناسب بهتے کے آن روز را نه سهو کنم / کے عسکرش شده با فوج انگلشی حامی

دلیر شکر او ست معین الخزرانی / دم مصاف بتاب و توان جنر غامی

در آن ستیز سمان شیر شاه بپو مرد

که بارها بمصاف و نبرد پا افشرد

Canto III. 8th & 9th Stanzas

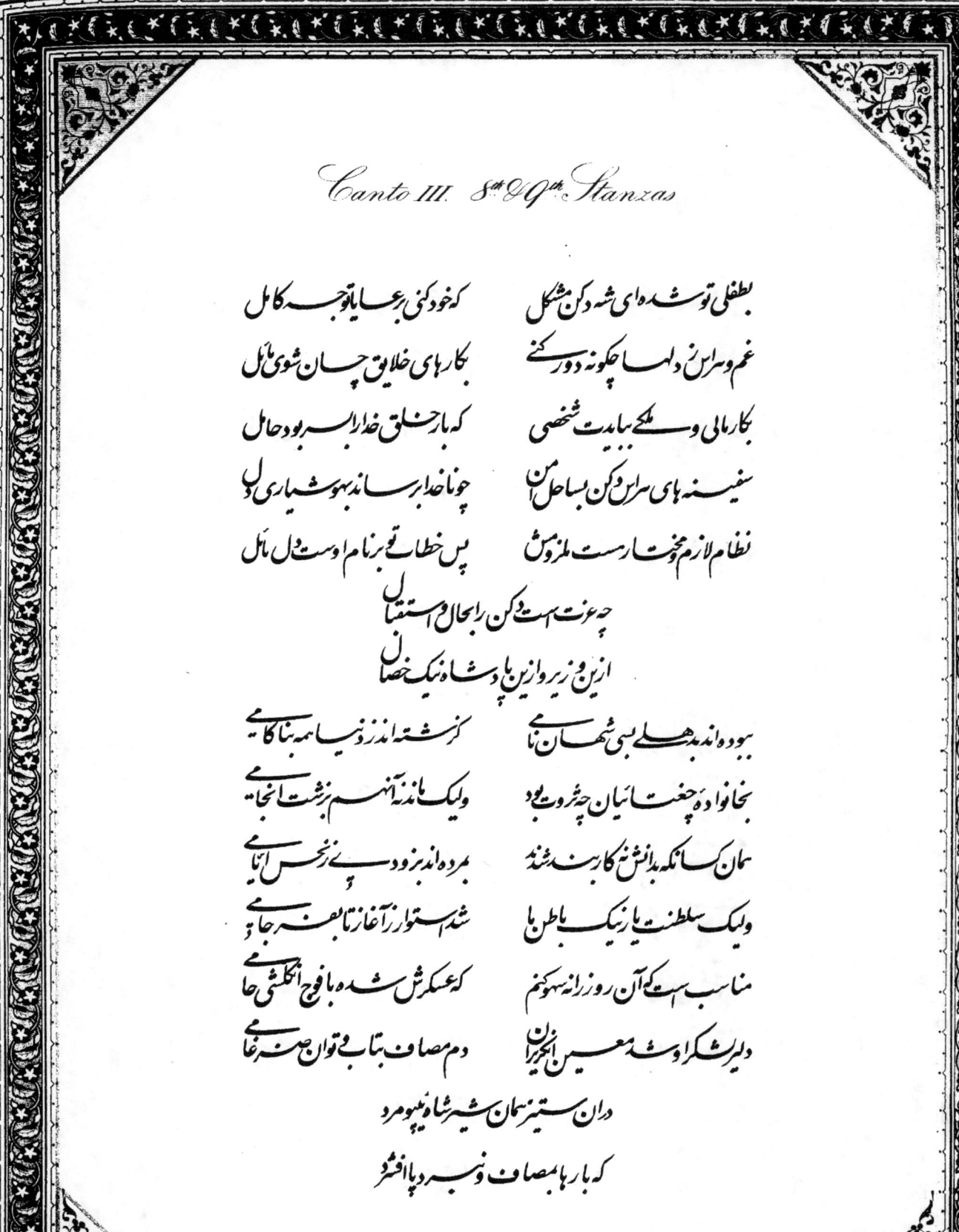

Canto III. 10th & 11th Stanzas

ازان نیمانه میدان کارزار منوز ستاده اند و عسلام کامکار منوز

درفش شکر انخیر نیرو نشان دکن بهمد کز نخستند و ستدار منوز

چو کشید بمند آتش مهیب عناد زشعله خیزی او مست خلق نار منوز

زبانه اش چپ بر والیان مندرسید بسوخت مند بماند و عنادار منوز

نظام ملک مسلح بجای خویش بماند مسلم است تا آتش بروز کار منوز

دم هر اس کسی که بیازموده شو

زد کران چراغتش فنزوده شو

بزرگ شاه نظام آنجنان دلاور کشت که با شجاعت او دیگری نمی کشت

بزور نیزه بر ان مرز بوم شد فروز که خوشنمای و وسعت در ان کشت

فر اختر زفر انس است ملک منقو حبث زبان آر او نافتح او فزون کشت

زوار داشته فیروز تا بغربی کات چو وارد اکسبے مرز و بوم از دست

چه کوه کات که چون خرب قلعه اش برید شفق بر آمده و شام با یک کشت

باین حدود چو ادبهر فتح عازمم

بسرزمین فر اخ از نصیب حاکم شد

Canto III. 12th & 13th Stanzas

چه طرفه شهر دریں قطعه حیدرآباد است ** که در دو شهر کوه کوه جنسر می زاد است

چه کوه است که ازسبزه کشته مینا کار ** چه چشمه است که مهر خورشید چهره بگشاد است

بپایه دومی در بلاد غربی هند ** سمین مقام مصنوعی خداداد است

بخطه دکن آن تختگاه در وسط است ** ملک بجمله دکن جسم و او دل شاد است

بعیش و ناز درنخبا مه سلمانان ** زشور و فتنه سمین فیا ملک آزاد است

چه سخت قلعه دریں تختگاه مرقو مست
که در خیل قوم دکرزان مقام ممنو عست

حصین تم ست ازین باره سنیک بارو ** میان کوی کبک دیده شد بوضع نکو

نبشته ست با فسانهای دیرینه ** که شاه سند درآباد بیش نمود غلو

نمود عزم که قوم و رعیت نخی درا ** بروز دهلی ودیگر مقام هار آنسو

بدو کسیر چو آن سخت باره نامی بود ** نه زینهار بماندد اصل سند در و

بر گذار هزاران ز درد جان فر سو ** بکام خود نرسید آخر آن شه بد جو

بضعف خلقت انسان نصیب سنجند
تباه سیخن دآن و شکرها که او بهند

Canto III. 12th & 13th Stanzas

چه طرفه شهر درین قطعه حیدرآباد است   که داور چو کهِ کوه جنس می زاد است

چه کوه است که از سبزه کشته مینا کار   چه چشمه ست که خورشید چهره بگشاد است

به پایهٔ دومی در بلاد عنبری هند   همین مقام نہ صنا عی خدا داد است

بخطّه دکن آن تختگاه در وسط است   ملک جملهٔ دکن جسم و او دل شاد است

بعیش و ناز دریں خطّہ نامه سلمانان   ز شور و فتنه زمین دار ملک آزاد است

چه سخت قلعه دریں تختگاه مرتفع است

که نسل قوم دکرزان مقام منتمی است

حصین تر است ازین بارهٔ نیک بارو   میان کوه نهنگ دیده شد بوضع نکو

نبشته ہیت با فسانهای دیرینه   که شاه ہند در آباد یش نمود غلو

نمود عزم که قوم و رعیت خمی درا   بروز دہلی و دیگر مقام ہا آنسو

بدیں کہ چون آن سخت بارہ نامی بود   نه تنہا رہاند دل اہل سند درو

برهگذار هزاران زور درد جانفزا   بکام خود رسید آخر آن شہ بدخو

بضعف خلقت انسان نصیب سنجند

تباه میکن آن ونکر ہا کہ اوبسند

Canto III. 14th & 15th Stanzas

چنان دیوکده از دیر باز ویران ماند   که در حصار حصینش شنید هیچ انسان ماند

زمین شنو که در نجا لعهد پیشینه   خروش فوج به نزدیکش فراوان ماند

دعای خلق جلاجل در آن چنان بخواست   که شهها مگر کشت و دید حیران ماند

درین بیان که توگفتم مبالغه نیست   بلی به هم سلف کار او بسامان ماند

زبیش و رس حاج زینت او بود   ولیک بعد ازان رنگ و نقش چنان ماند

به پیش از آنکه شود شهرت مسائل دینا

بدیوکیه بماند نے و نق و آد ین

قریب دیوکده آن شهر خوب شد واقع   که جای اوست بیک کوشائے و بشاع

گران حصار چو شوست این چپا بنیت   که است غفت بر شوی فرخی طالع

فقط بملک دکن نیست نام او مشهو   که خویش بم یار کرس شش شائے

چه شهرست که مردم تجاره کویت   مکن کنج فشان نام اوست بر ساع

چه بلده بود که مشهد و دولت او شد

بواقعات بسا نام و شهرت او شد

Canto III. 16th & 17th Stanzas

چو کنج نیست تجاره کنون بویرانه   نه قصه ایست در اینجا هیچ کاشانه

قریب اوست کسی کو به نقصان مشو   قتاده هست بر و آنخی نه بخانه

کزاز شنیدن نامش شهان سراسیمه کنند   اگر چه گفته شود در میان فسانه

ز خاندان معلوم و دان شفیحا   که نام اوشد اورنگ می دا

بطوف کوه صنم خانهای و برسل   که صنع شانج در آید بعقل من نرا

نه در ولایت یونان نظیر آن بنی

نه در قلم و مصر آنچنان مکان بنی

چه املا حسرفه در این کج و محنتی کند   که سالهانه در انجا کسانی کردند

کسی کم شده آن کم مجوسته آنا   مگر ز جان بهمین کالفتی کند

نبوده اند به تعمیر صرف صناعان   بسی کسان عیت چه مستی کند

که عاجزان و علیلان مثال موم دنیا   هزار سال برایش کلاتی کردند

میان کوه صنم خانها بجستند   همه زیاده ز فرهاد دستی کردند

نه از کمین پلنگان و شیر ترسیدند   نه از گزند سیه مار بستی کردند

نه جوع و عطش کسی ز انیان بدل شد

نه از شتاو نه از صی نه هیچ کامل شد

Canto III. 18th & 19th Stanzas

گشت آئینه بندهات و فرنگ بسی $\qquad$ ز تاب می در انجاست نیب و نک بسی

بفرش سنگ خامش تابخ سرو $\qquad$ مثال قوس قزح دیده ایم تاک بسی

بدیرهای اولی از آن کسائی خواب $\qquad$ شدست صرف رو وقت وجه ترنگ بسی

و کر مقابل هم این و آن بهم سخن $\qquad$ کند فرنگ نا قلیم سنت نگ بسی

چو دیر و صومعه باشند فی المثال و فی البر

به پوییش و دین و آن فتد در پس

عجیب تر جبلی و یکجا از جنس نیست $\qquad$ در این دره کز نوع انس حاشا نیست

به سنگلاخ چها غار تیره و تار است $\qquad$ که جز سباع و کرجانور در انجا نیست

از ان کسانکه نخست اندر ان سفر کردند $\qquad$ کسی دگر چو آنان و اصل دنیا نیست

بعد کرچو سپرهاست این جبال تمام $\qquad$ درون فتد در آنکه مرد سحا نیست

محال است بهر کس به برون رفتن $\qquad$ پیچ پیچ این کوه جاده نیست

چنانکه جس و انفاس نشر مسکرا

در این جبال بمان قیمه بهره پیدا

Canto III. 20th & 21st Stanzas

درین طریق و ره تاریکی شتاب مکن   بدشت و وادی پرخار اضطراب مکن

چنین مباد که بأیت بما زخسته فتد   ورا بهوش میار و بخود عذاب مکن

و یا که خفته دوی ناگهان شیخ دعا   تو در شتاب وی و کار تو خراب مکن

بدان تشنه برین و دآب می تشنند   برو گذار تو زنهار بهر آب مکن

بوقت و زدریخا کمال خاشیوست   ظلمت شب اینجا کمی حساب مکن

بجوف ناک صدا ها دلم چو لرزیدہ   قدم بره منه و نیز میل خواب مکن

اگر چه کوه ازین نعره ها بشور آید

ولیک مرد چسری را دران سکون باید

بران مقام که آن تیره رود آخر شد   نظر بلند کن و بین که طرفه صادر شد

چه دیرها و چها غارها متصل اینجاست   که کارخیه بروی جبال ظاهر شد

مگر گروه پری کرده این شکفتها   که زین بدایع خوش عقل انس فاتر شد

شمرده اند همین کوہ را پر از برکت   که تکیه گاه سازاهان صابر شد

نروی داد چنین سیر گاه در دنیا   نه زینها عیان کسی مسافر شد

نه در خیال بیاید چنین سر پُشکاہ

نه بهر اهل دلان مجا و سبحاپی پناہ

Canto III. 22nd & 23rd Stanzas

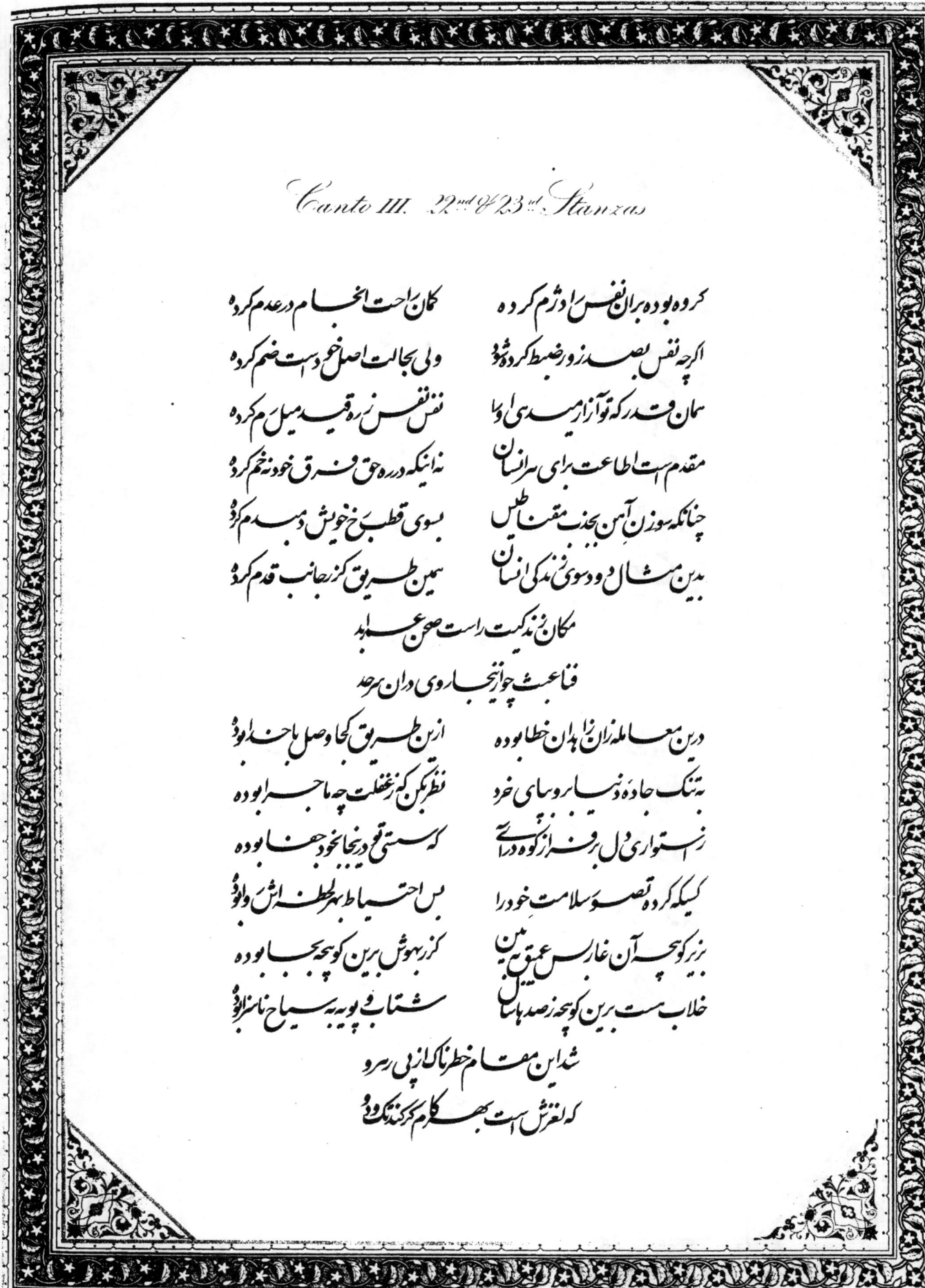

Canto III. 21st & 25th Stanzas

بسی معابد خوب و فراخ چرخ مثال   نه خاور اندرسوی باخته بشکل هلال

مثال سایه و شخص اندر سوی برو آن   بپیش مهر و پس مهر بهای خوش تمثال

بغرب کوی یکی آبشار می ریزد   همین مقام خطرگاه ره‌روست کما ل

نه پیچ پشتی شده انجام هاشم و نافع   که افتاد بن و مانده جناب لحوا ل

بپیچ پیچ مش کنے کز اک کنه   بنا کزرفت ره رو بعنا روبا ل

بنا چگونه نه شد این خوبتر عمارتها

کجا مثال غل زها د و این صناعتها

منبت اند بابواب و بساپیکر   بشکل دیو مهیب و ولی نیک سیر

درون قصر برین کوه پیکر ستاست   که کاندو تواند کشید از و بهمته

کشیده است چه تصویر خیل ماه رخان   که خفته چشم نیایند و موی شان از زر

حقیقت اینکه دل آنخی همی لند   که کرده است درین کارنامه خوش نظر

چه مثل است درین جلوه گاه صبر و سکو ن   چه آفت است بجان و دلش درین منظر

چگونه پاک نظر بوده از و فور حیا

چگونه صاف دلش مانده از شرو ر هوا

Canto III. 26th & 27th Stanzas

مثال وضع خلقتـش سر در ودیوار   سپیدو چهـره وار زق نزهت اقلا

کشیده است بر ان نقش صـورت کلهــا   برای اهل تماشاشده ست تازه هـا

که کرده است درینجا صنایع بی مثـل   کدام ساخته سر و عجیب نقش و نگــا

بناکزیرینی آدمـی بس حیــران   ازین مقـام شکفتـی فـتـاده طلع آنـا

گذشـته هست بر ود و هزار سال الیک   ر صنعتش نشد آگـاه هیچ نادره کا

مگر نبود چنیـن عقـل هیـچ انسـان یا

که اکتساب کند پیشـه زرکــان یـا

چه گویم از همـه اعجوبـه های ملک ختـن   زبان یکی و صد هنا ها ببینـــه بـین

هم رز و بوم فراخش چه نادر اشیاست   همـه عظیـم و همـه خوشنـما می حسـن

چـه چشمها ست مصفــا چـه دشـت هــاد   چه رود ست بکوه و بریک لطمه زن

بسر دو دیده به بحـر محیط خسرو خویش   که تا خراج دهـد زاب صافـی رو شن

تمام خوبتر اشیــا وقت درقی انجــات   زوی حیاتـی ز رو نسـه کی واز معـن

همه نظمـه بتوای شـاه نـوجـوان دارنـد

که حکم تو رسد و بالو بـب جـا آرنـد

Canto III. 28th & 29th Stanzas

خوشـا جلوس تو بوده ببارگاه عظیم / با ولیـن درجه هـمچو شـاه با عظیم

بـبوی تو نخـران دیده هـای مجلسیـان / که جلوه ثـابت تجـاه خـاص ولطف عمیـم

باین صغـیر سنے دتو وآن تهذیب / کـه مدح کـوی تو بـود نـد حاسدان لئیـم

کنـون بناصیـه ات آن جـلال وشـوکـت / که بر سر تو سـزد ایـست خسـروی هـم

چو اکتسـاب کنـی خلق و عـلم شاهانه / نظیـر تو بود اندر دیار مـن عـدیم

همـه فضـائل نـیکـو بـدل نهان داری

جمـال نـیـز چـو شاهان بـبی عیـان داری

چنـان نشسـتـه تو بـودی بپیـش شـاهی تخـت / که میـل کرده بـسوی تو دیده هـای بخـت

چـهـرهٔ تـو عـیـان بـود وآن صـفای دل / کـه زینـهـار نـداری نظـر جـاه و تخـت

مسـلم اسـت بـه نـزد خسـرو دوران ایـن امـر / که شاهـکان ادب بـوده به تخـت و بـدر

دلـی زصـاف درونـی نـخـوتی کـرد و / بـبارگـاه نـمـودی حسـین تـوجـه سخـت

کـه لفـظ لفـظ کنی یاد قیصـری پیغـام / بـیچ سـیـنـه بـداری هـمـیـن شهـانـه بخـت

محـبـتی کـه زانگـلـن کـرده حـاصـل

ازیـن پـیـام همیـشـه فـزون کنـی در دل

Canto III. 30th Stanza

نبشته شد چو با نگلش چنین بیان متین   زقله سنوک فاضل جلیل ترین

بحکم عالی کرنل ذیوس شاه ملو   به نظم پارسی این تجانه زرنگین

سه ماه و بی این کار رفت در دو ملے   بلطف حاکم خود هائید بابین تمکین

چه غوطها بزده دریم تفکر ژرف   بدست خویش بیاوردہم چنین

قیض وحی استاد غالب منفور   زعون علم امیر زمان ضیاءالدین

چه کاوکاو نمودم بگنج خانهٔ دل   چه زر و درو گهر یافتم زبخت معین

بدرج پارسی آن سلک گوهر نگلش   زاحتیاط نهادم من وآئی کین

چو ساختم نی تایخ او بدل اینک   هدایتی شده اکه مرا بجهر دو شنین

بگوگه نغمه عقل ایت این سفینه سود

کتاب زمزمه قصیده یست پنجم

کتبه ذرهٔ خاکسار محمد رحیم بیک ولد میرزا عبید الله بیک